When you hear Steve speak and you ask him questions and hear his response and then see with your eyes the kind of work Steve's involved in, you can't help but begin to think that the tomb may, in fact, be empty.

Rob Bell, Mars Hill Bible Church

Apprentice is a story-filled and helpful roadmap for the journey toward God.

John Ortberg, pastor and author,
Menlo Park Presbyterian Church

A delectable read, like candy for the soul. *Apprentice* is winsome, poetic, intelligent and sassy. Steve Chalke reminds us that at the core of disciple is discipline, and that means training ourselves in the divine arts — love, forgiveness, peace, grace, justice.

Shane Claiborne, author,
Jesus for President

I've said this before, and perhaps I'll say it again, but I think this is Steve Chalke's best book ever.... Steve Chalke and Joanna Wyld have given us the best short introduction to life in the way of Jesus that I've ever come across: it's simple yet deep, short yet comprehensive. And the mini-parables that fill the book will get stuck in your imagination in the best way possible.

Brian McLaren, author/networker,
brianmclaren.net

Steve amazes us with an array of wonderful stories and brilliant quotes that we shall long remember and often use. Imitating Jesus, he gives us parables that profoundly affect how we look at like and journey on life's way.

Tony Campolo, Ph.D., Eastern University

In this highly accessible book Steve takes complex truths about discipleship and unpacks them in a way that is both 'action' provoking and inspiring. His honest rhetoric and anecdotal delivery makes this a must-read for those of us who are serious [illegible]s that reflect the essence of God [illegible]

Also by Steve Chalke

Change Agents: 25 Hard-Learned Lessons in the Art of Getting Things Done

Intelligent Church: A Journey Towards Christ-Centred Community (with Anthony Watkis)

The Lost Message of Jesus (with Alan Mann)

apprentice

walking the way of Christ

STEVE CHALKE

with JOANNA WYLD

ZONDERVAN®

ZONDERVAN

Apprentice
Copyright © 2009 by Steve Chalke
Requests for information should be addressed to:

Zondervan, *Grand Rapids, Michigan 49530*

Library of Congress Cataloging-in-Publication Data

Chalke, Steve.
Apprentice : walking the way of Christ / Steve Chalke, with Joanna Wyld.
p. cm.
Includes bibliographical references.
ISBN 978-0-310-29154-1 (softcover)
1. Christian life. 2. Spiritual life--Christianity. 3. Spirituality. I. Wyld, Joanna. II. Title.
BV4501.3.C426 2009
248.4--dc22

Steve Chalke asserts the moral right to be identified as the author of this book.

All Scripture quotations, unless otherwise indicated, are taken from the *Holy Bible, New International Version*®. NIV®. Copyright © 1973, 1978, 1984 by International Bible Society. Used by permission of Zondervan. All rights reserved. Scripture quotations marked CEV are taken from the Contemporary English Version. Copyright © 1995 by American Bible Society. Used by permission. Scripture quotations marked The Message are taken from *The Message*. Copyright © 1993, 1994, 1995, 1996, 2000, 2001, 2002. Used by permission of NavPress Publishing Group. Scripture quotations marked NASB are taken from the *New American Standard Bible*. Copyright © 1960, 1962, 1963, 1968, 1971, 1972, 1973, 1975, 1977, 1995 by The Lockman Foundation. Used by permission. Scripture quotations marked WE are taken from The Bible in Worldwide English (New Testament) published in 1996 by SOON Educational Publications.

Any Internet addresses (websites, blogs, etc.) and telephone numbers printed in this book are offered as a resource. They are not intended in any way to be or imply an endorsement by Zondervan, nor does Zondervan vouch for the content of these sites and numbers for the life of this book.

All rights reserved. No part of this publication may be reproduced, stored in a retrieval system, or transmitted in any form or by any means - electronic, mechanical, photocopy, recording, or any other - except for brief quotations in printed reviews, without the prior permission of the publisher.

Interior design by Ben Fetterley

Printed in the United States of America

09 10 11 12 13 • 23 22 21 20 19 18 17 16 15 14 13 12 11 10 9 8 7 6 5 4 3 2 1

CONTENTS

Acknowledgements *7*

1 Journeying 9

2 Longing 29

3 Believing 45

4 Questioning 61

5 Belonging 79

6 Serving 95

7 Persevering 111

8 Forgiving 129

9 Listening 147

10 Engaging 165

Notes *185*

ACKNOWLEDGEMENTS

Steve and Joanna would like to thank Sue Robbins, Judith Doel, Ro Leech, Jill Rowe, Joe Davis, Julian Mines, Daniel Castro, Matt Clayton, Kate, Colin, Richard and Andrew Wyld for their inspiration as we have written this book, but most of all Eva for making Joanna laugh.

Steve also wants to acknowledge his indebtedness to all those who have inspired and shaped his thinking as they have written or spoken of their journey with Christ. To borrow again, from Kenneth Schmitz, himself quoted by Stanley Hauerwas: "I cannot make use of the simplest technique which did not have to be discovered and brought to excellence by nameless craftsmen; so that most of my benefactors remain unknown to me. Some of us can name a few generations of our ancestors, but before long the chain of those who have helped to give us life fades into obscurity."[1]

So, to those apprentices of Christ, both known and unknown, past and present, thank you.

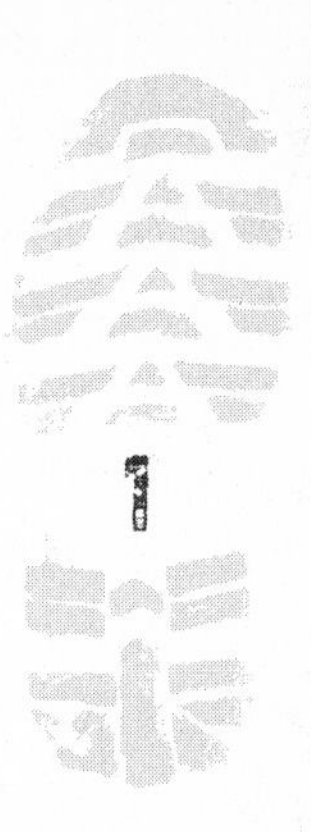

1

JOURNEYING

A man once dreamt of leaving his home to go in search of the Golden City, which lay on the other side of a vast forest. His own life was tedious. He had grown tired of his surroundings, responsibilities and relationships. No one in his town had ever been to the Golden City, but the tales of its size and beauty had been told for generations.

Eventually, his desire to experience this wonderful place for himself became irresistible. So one morning, the man woke early and, after saying goodbye to his wife and young children, set out on his journey of discovery.

The man travelled for many hours, slowly making his way through the dense forest that separated his own town from the Golden City. He had no idea how long his journey would take nor what might await him at its end. But his determination to keep going was constantly fuelled by the inspirational stories he had heard of his intended destination. Eventually, despite his great enthusiasm, he became overwhelmed by exhaustion. So, finding a clearing, he settled down under a large tree to rest.

However, not wanting to awaken disoriented and so lose his direction, he took off his shoes and laid them side by side, pointing in the direction he was travelling. Assured that he would now avoid getting lost, he closed his eyes and fell into a deep sleep.

But while he slept, two young boys out playing in the forest entered the clearing and stumbled across him. Seeing the man asleep and his shoes lying neatly beside him, they decided to play a trick on him. Silently, they crept closer to him with the intent of hiding his shoes. But just as one of the boys picked them up and turned to retreat, he stepped on a dry twig which cracked beneath his foot. The man began to stir. Startled, the boy hurriedly dropped the shoes and, with his friend, fled. The man half woke, sat upright, and blearily looked around him, but, seeing nothing, soon went back to sleep.

Early the following morning, the man awoke and, carefully putting on his shoes so that they continued to point in what he thought was the same direction, he set off once more. He walked for the whole day until finally, as dusk fell, he came to the edge of the forest, and there, before his very eyes, at last, was the Golden City.

As he got closer, the man began to feel strangely at home. Things here were exactly as he had imagined. It wasn't that the city was any bigger than his own, but he had a strong feeling of belonging–a sense of coming home. His eyes lit up as he walked past what felt like familiar shops and houses.

But best of all, he came across a very familiar street where he found a familiar house. He knocked on a familiar door and was greeted by a familiar-looking family. He smiled a deep smile because he felt at peace. And he thanked God that after his long and difficult journey, he had finally reached his destination.[1]

Life is a journey.

But is this journey just an aimless meandering, or is it something more? Are we merely drifting through each year as it passes, or dare we hope that life is a journey with purpose and a destination?

For much of our lives, we repress such difficult questions. Instead, we fill our time with frenetic distractions and diverting amusements.

However, every now and then–perhaps over a meal or a drink with a friend of many years; or disturbed by a long, sleepless night; or faced with a personal difficulty or family tragedy; or gazing up at the moon and countless stars on a clear summer's night–the questions find a way of breaking through.

One way or another, life's awkward questions have a habit of catching up with us.

Much of life's journey, it turns out, is a quest to find ourselves and our place in the world. The journey of life is a process of self-discovery.

Each one of us needs a convincing story which tells us who we are, an overarching narrative with structure, purpose and direction. For, without a story–a sense of who we are and how we fit in–we are lost. At best we survive, but we will never thrive.

Many choose to fill the void left by the absence of a story with the pursuit of money, sex or power. Yet it is still apparent that the real search, even then, is for the deeper treasures of security, love and a sense of significance.

Furthermore, when we are ensnared by the dizzying dance of life, blinded in its glittering glare, our sense of being lost is magnified. Yet this sense of 'lostness' should never be despised. It can be a wonderful gift. The realisation that we are lost brims with hope and opportunity. For this very sense of being lost, when embraced rather than ignored, can become the impetus that spurs us on to take the next step forward on our journey.

THE QUEST FOR MEANING

In the movie *The Motorcycle Diaries*, the young Ernesto 'Che' Guevara and his friend Alberto Granado embark on an epic journey across South America. They begin in high spirits, but their travels bring into focus disturbing questions about life. At one point, Guevara sums up the nature of journeying in this way: 'Each moment seems split in two: melancholy for what is left behind and the excitement of entering a new land.'[2]

The two men encounter extremes of weather and constant danger; their motorbike fails; they fall ill and struggle to find shelter and food. But they also discover new priorities through encountering communities stricken by poverty, prejudice and gross social injustice–experiences that form the social idealism for which they would eventually become famous. As Guevara observes: 'We could feel the world changing ... or was it us?'[3]

A journey of any length will take in many landscapes, not all of which will be beautiful and awe-inspiring. But, though life is often tedious or even treacherous, each experience remains an integral part of the journey.

If a journey implies a destination, then a destination implies a direction, and a direction implies decisions. But every decision we make entails the limiting of options. To choose one road, we must reject another. As Thomas Aquinas observed, 'Every choice is a renunciation.' Which means that to move forward with a genuine sense of purpose and direction, we must make sacrifices.

Perhaps that is why ambling through life, ignoring these questions, appears, to so many, to be the easiest option.

While we are more than happy to accept the joys and the highs, the successes and the good times of life, we constantly question the pain, the sorrow and the suffering. Yet these too have important lessons to teach us. And because life is a journey rather than a guided tour, we have to be alert to any clues we might find along our path, even when they come to us through the medium of pain and disappointment. Ignoring these clues will leave us impoverished.

Only by learning to negotiate life's peaks and troughs can we progress on our journey. It is as we wrestle with the never-ending questions that we move forward, and only through searching can we find our way.

> To get through the hardest journey we need take only one step at a time, but we must keep on stepping.
>
> CHINESE PROVERB

As we search, we find that some questions trouble us more persistently than others. Above all, there's that big, disturbing question that keeps resurfacing. It's the question encapsulated in the lyrics of countless songs, the lines of poems and the scripts of new movies each year. It's found on the lips and in the thoughts of millions of people around the world, even as you are reading these words:

Why?

Homo sapiens are, by nature, meaning-seeking creatures. And, of all the questions we ever ask, the most important has to be: Why am I here? The advances of science have done a wonderful job of telling me *what I am*. But, in order to thrive I also need to know *who I am*, and, even more fundamentally, *why I am*.

'Do I matter? What should I do with my life? What have I done with my life?'

'Have I blown it? Is there any hope for me?'

'Am I loved?'

'Am I lovable?'

'What's the point?'

'Does my life count?'

From the statesman to the street kid, these are the questions that shout to us in our pain and whisper to us in our most honest moments.

This quest for meaning, for identity, is the pursuit of every man and every woman in every age.

> Who is it that can tell me who I am?
>
> WILLIAM SHAKESPEARE, *KING LEAR*

SEARCHING FOR ANSWERS

Some claim there is no meaning. They say there is no answer to the big question.

'The universe that we observe has precisely the properties we should expect if there is, at bottom, no design, no purpose, no evil and no good, nothing but blind, pitiless indifference,'[4] claims Professor Richard Dawkins.

The philosopher Bertrand Russell similarly asserted: 'The universe is just there, and that's all.' To which the Jesuit priest F. W. Copleston responded, in a now famous radio debate with Russell, that in stating the obvious, that the universe exists–which nobody is denying–Russell was effectively refusing to engage in a debate on the big question: Why?[5]

'The first question which should rightly be asked,' wrote philosopher G. W. F. Leibniz, is this: 'Why is there something rather than nothing?'[6]

More recently, songwriter Martyn Joseph explored the value of asking the big questions in his song 'Treasure the Questions':

> *Searching Saharas of sorrow*
> *Trying to understand why*
> *But the journey has brought me so much closer,*
> *I don't have to stand here and lie*
> *Over and over I cried in the darkness*
> *Over and over to see*
> *The crime is to sit and not wonder*
> *Renewing my mind set me free*[7]

In the end, the deepest questions we all ask–from president to priest–are not those to do with science or the relentless search for facts, but those to do with theology:[8] our thoughts and words about God. We want to know if there is meaning and, if so, how that meaning affects our place in the universe, our purpose in life, our actions and our relationships. As Erwin Raphael McManus puts it: 'The human story seems more driven by the insanity of love than the survival of the fittest.'[9]

Jesuit philosopher Anthony de Mello wrote:

> The genius of a composer is found in the notes of his music; but analysing the notes will not reveal his genius. The poet's greatness is contained in his

> words; yet the study of his words will not disclose his inspiration. God reveals himself in creation; but scrutinize creation as minutely as you wish, you will not find God, any more than you will find the soul through careful examination of your body.[10]

If there is no God, then any purpose we give to our lives, and our journey through it, is one that we've necessarily invented and imposed. If there is no God, then we are all just 'lost in space'.

But what if the universe is personal? What if our lives are more than the result of time and chance?

MOVING FORWARD

With its first four majestic words, the Bible declares, 'In the beginning, God ...'

What if that statement is true?

If true, these words are utterly transformational of all else. Behind life, the universe and the whole of existence is a personal being, a Creator. The universe becomes pregnant with purpose. If creation is the intentional work of a personal God, then it has intrinsic meaning and our lives have purpose within it.

Life was wonderful in the small village that nestled in the bottom of the deep valley alongside the clear, fast-flowing waters of the river.

The river gave life to the village, providing fresh water for drinking and washing as well as irrigation for the land. It was also a rich source of food.

Each year the villagers gather in the community hall to give thanks for the river.

On one such occasion, a young man stood up to address the people. 'The river brings life to our village. But I intend to go in search of its source.'

The people were shocked. No one had ever travelled to the source of the river. It was thought to be far too long and dangerous a journey to undertake. They tried to dissuade the young man, but without success. The following morning, he set out on his journey, confident that he would succeed and return to tell them where the river began.

The weeks soon turned into months, the seasons changed and the harsh winter set in without any word of the young explorer. Doubts turned to certainty that he had perished, and the people's thoughts about the source of the river died with him.

Then, on the first anniversary of his departure, the people gathered, as was their annual tradition, to celebrate the life of the river. But during the celebrations, much to their surprise, the doors of the community hall were flung open and there, standing in the entrance, was the young man.

'I've been to the source!' he shouted at the top of his voice. The villagers were ecstatic. They dragged him to the heart of the hall and gathered around him.

'The river rises in mountains many months from here. As it makes its way, it is joined by many tributaries that feed other villages just like ours. There are waterfalls and rapids to traverse and many landscapes that it passes through.' As he spoke, he drew a crude map of his journey on a tablecloth.

Within days, the story was being recounted all over the village. The map had been copied and printed and was now on sale in local shops. At every opportunity, the villagers asked him more questions about his journey to the source of the river.

Eventually his story was written down, an official guide to the journey to the river source was produced as well as numerous poems, songs, paintings and books retelling the young man's story.

But from that day to this, no one else has ever travelled to the source of the river. It's still considered far too dangerous a journey to undertake.

Some of us begin the journey well, but along the way we become overwhelmed by the responsibilities of life and end up travelling blindly, without purpose or direction. It becomes all too easy for us to neglect what is vital in the midst of what is demanded. Life was once an adventure to be lived. But, somewhere along the way, we lost our capacity for wonder. We feel trapped in a moribund world of routine.

Sometimes people stagnate, or are immobilised, because of a bad experience. Pain and bitterness slowly form a cocoon in which the wounded individual is encased. They inhabit it and feed on it for the rest of their life.

Others stagnate for the opposite reason. They are stopped in their tracks by a religious experience, a professional achievement or the heady freedom of youth, and they cannot move forward. By this experience, all else is measured. The remainder of their journey is spent trying to recreate the past rather than pressing on into the future.

Both of these routes are dead-ends. The future and the present are sacrificed, and the past dominates our field of vision. But experiences are like the wind; we cannot bottle them. Instead, we have to keep moving forward.

However much we wish we could step back in time, undo the things we feel have robbed us of the life we have hoped for, correct the mistakes we have made or re-negotiate the wrong turnings and dead-ends that we have taken, the reality is: we can't.

After several hours of travelling, a young man finally arrived at the city he'd been journeying towards. He was there to visit a group of friends, but soon realised that finding their house wasn't going to be an easy task–even with a map. After what seemed like hours of searching, exhausted, dejected, frustrated and totally disoriented, he approached a middle-aged woman to ask the way. The woman looked surprised and bemused by the request. For a moment or two she gazed quizzically at the man before replying, 'I know exactly where you want to get to, but if I was going to travel there, I wouldn't start from here.'

Each one of us must begin the next stage of our journey from where we are, however lost or far from home we may feel. There is no alternative.

LEARNING ON THE MOVE

Jesus was a rabbi (the ancient Hebrew word for 'teacher').[11] And, like other rabbis before him, he gathered apprentices, or *talmidim*,[12] to him, to live alongside him and learn through practice.

An ap·pren·tice is:

1. One who is learning by practical experience under skilled workers a trade, art or calling.
2. A beginner, a learner, an inexperienced person, a novice.

The rabbinic teaching style did not primarily consist of attending lectures or sermons and reading texts. Jesus' first followers were apprentices – theirs was a whole-life, active experience. Their learning was varied and diverse, deep and profound. Jesus' disciples learned from him not just through formal instruction but through observation, imitation and practice. There were misunderstandings and mistakes. There were setbacks and successes. They formed habits and skills by watching their teacher, reflecting on his words, learning from his actions and practising for themselves.

But, more than this, Jesus required a personal commitment from his disciples founded on service as a way of getting to know their rabbi's way of life. The rabbi's knowledge could only be passed on from life to life. Rabbis had no interest in having a student spit back information just for information's sake. They wanted to know if a student understood the teaching and had wrestled with and engaged with it on a personal level.

Becoming the apprentice of a rabbi in the first century was, therefore, quite different from the experience of a typical twenty-first-century student.

Today, students want to *know* what their teacher *knows* so they can achieve a grade, complete a course or pass an exam.

In contrast with this, a first-century apprentice wanted to *be* like their teacher–to *become* what the teacher was.

The ancient rabbis taught on the move. Learning was literally a journey. Life for every rabbi's apprentice became a real journey of learning. With a rabbi, the whole of life became a risk-taking, active experience, often entailing leaving the security of home and venturing wherever the rabbi decided to go. Jesus' first apprentices 'left everything and followed him' (Luke 5:11).

Jesus taught out and about, on the streets, in the marketplace, the temple courtyard and on the mountainside. He gave lessons in the countryside, around meal tables and on the lake shore. And, because the most profound learning engages all five senses–hearing, sight, touch, taste and smell–Jesus often created multi-sensory learning environments in order that people might more fully comprehend his message. In his book *Wise Teaching*, Charles F. Melchert described it this way:

> Jesus' apprentice-disciples did learn concepts and beliefs but also shared emotions, attitudes, dispositions, behaviours, anxieties, uncertainties, hopes, and loyalties. All these were intertwined with certain smells, the taste of bread, and fish, the rocky road beneath the feet, the rocking of the boat, and the still quiet at night. Learning in this manner would reach more levels of character and consciousness than the linguistic mastery of contemporary schooling.[13]

A talmid followed the rabbi everywhere, every day and every hour of the day–often without knowing or asking where he was going–with one simple goal: to imitate him.

The rabbi-talmid relationship is famously portrayed in the ancient Hebrew document known as the Mishnah.[14] The Mishnah teaches apprentices how to follow a rabbi: 'You should become dusty in the dust of their feet; and you should imbibe their words thirstily.'[15] Whenever you would see a rabbi, you would find a group of his apprentices walking behind him, doing their best to keep up with him as he walked and taught. After a long day of travelling directly behind their rabbi, the students would be covered in the dust flicked up by his sandals.

A rabbi's apprentice rarely left his teacher's side for fear that he would miss a teachable moment. He watched his rabbi's every move, noting how he acted and thought in any given situation. Apprentices trusted their rabbi completely and worked passionately to incorporate his actions and attitudes, as well as his words, into their lives. A disciple's deepest desire was to follow his rabbi so closely that he would start to think, and act, just like him.

Many Jewish scholars believe that this offers the best understanding of how Peter (one of Jesus' first disciples) briefly walked on water. When Jesus (the rabbi) was seen walking out on the lake, Peter (the talmid) felt the need to imitate his rabbi (see Matthew 14:22–33).

Understanding Jesus in his role as a rabbi also gives us a much clearer sense of his resonant phrase: 'Come, follow me' (Matthew 4:19). Jesus wasn't just inviting people for a short walk down to the beach; he was calling them to imitate his way of life. If they accepted his challenge, they would spend the next years of their lives learning to walk in the way of Jesus, literally following in his footsteps.

Jesus, like other rabbis, often employed stories and parables to engage his apprentices in the learning process because it forced them to think more deeply and work out for themselves an appropriate response. Typically, when Jesus was asked a question, he did not respond by reasoning from a starting point to a conclusion. Rather, he would reply by telling a story, by engaging his audience and by getting them involved in arriving at the answer in a vivid and personal way.

In essence, Jesus would say: 'Do you want to find meaning? Then I won't bore you with philosophical arguments or theological and dogmatic statements. Instead, I'll tell you a story. I'll ask you a question. And I'll provoke you with my attitudes and actions.'

A good story is a window. A picture that opens into another realm. A glimpse into a bigger world. Sometimes it can even be a mirror. A story can show us ourselves.

Having told his story, very often Jesus would just leave it there. Hanging. Jesus would often leave his stories unexplained, allowing his listeners the freedom to explore his ideas independently.

'What shall we say the kingdom of God[16] is like, or what parable shall we use to describe it?' he said. 'It is like a mustard seed, which is the smallest seed you plant in the ground. Yet when planted, it grows and becomes the largest of all garden plants, with such big branches that the birds of the air can perch in its shade' (Mark 4:30–32).

And so Jesus planted another seed, a seed which can, if nurtured, take root and grow in our lives.

To become an apprentice of Christ, we must allow him to stimulate our thinking and shape our responses, just as he did for his first followers two millennia ago. Even when it calls us to leave comfort behind, make sacrifices and take risks.

Jesus told another parable: 'Again, the kingdom of heaven[17] is like a merchant looking for fine pearls. When he found one of great value, he went away and sold everything he had and bought it' (Matthew 13:45–46).

'I want this pearl. How much is it?'

'Well,' the seller says, 'it's very expensive.'

'But how much?' the apprentice asks.

'Well, a very large amount.'

'Do you think I could buy it?'

'Oh, of course. Everyone can buy it.'

'But didn't you say it was very expensive?'

'Yes.'

'Well, how much is it?'

'Everything you have,' says the seller.

The apprentice pauses and thinks. But the pearl is of great quality. He makes up his mind.

'All right, I'll buy it,' he says.

'Well, what do you have?' the seller wants to know. 'Let's write it down.'

'Well, I have ten thousand pounds in the bank.'

'Good–ten thousand pounds. What else?'

'That's all. That's all I have.'

'Nothing more?'

'Well, I have a few pounds–some loose change–here in my pockets.'

'How much?'

The apprentice starts digging. 'Well, let's see–five, ten, twenty, twenty-two, twenty-five pounds.'

'That's good. What else do you have?'

'Nothing. Nothing at all. That's it.'

'Where do you live?' He's still probing.

'In a house, on the other side of town.'

'The house too then.' He writes that down.

'You mean I have to live in my caravan?'

'You have a caravan? Good. That too. What else?'

'But . . . but that means I'll have to sleep in my car!'

'You have a car as well?'

'Well, two actually.'

'Both become mine, both cars. Anything else?'

'Well, you already have my money, my house, my caravan, my cars. What more do you want? I have absolutely nothing left! I am totally alone now.'

Suddenly the seller exclaims, 'Oh, I almost forgot! You yourself too! Everything becomes mine. House, money, cars–and you too.'[18]

Apprenticeship is not about half-measures. It involves perseverance, practice, dedication and the readiness to learn. It means investing our passion, our talents and our whole selves. But the rewards are beyond price. And the resultant journey is the most thrilling adventure we will ever experience.

As the poet Ted Hughes wrote in a letter to his son, Nicholas, 'The only calibration that counts is how much heart people invest, how much they ignore their fears of being hurt or caught out or humiliated. And the only thing people regret is that they didn't live boldly enough, that they didn't invest enough heart, didn't love enough.'[19]

Live boldly.

As it was said to the blind man Bartimaeus as Jesus passed through his town (see Mark chapter 10):

'Cheer up! On your feet! He's calling you.'

2

LONGING

I have never really accepted what I am—a forty-five-year-old man, working in a grocery store in a small town, married to a good if unexciting woman, aware that my marriage will never fulfil my deep sexual yearnings, and aware that, despite all my daydreaming and hopes to the contrary, I am not going anywhere. I will never fulfil my dreams; I will only be here, as I am now, in this small town, in this particular marriage, with these people, in this body, for the rest of my life. I will only grow fatter, balder, and physically less healthy and attractive. But what is sad in all of this is that from every indication, I should be having a good life. I am healthy, loved, secure, in a good marriage, living in a country of peace and plenty. Yet, inside myself I am so restless that I never enjoy my life and my wife and my kids and my job and the place that I live in. I am always at some other place inside myself, too restless to be where I am, too restless to live in my own house, too restless to be inside my own skin.[1]

As Erwin Raphael McManus put it: 'My soul craves, but for what I don't know.'[2]

Very often, we direct this indefinable, ongoing longing into short-term cravings that grow out of our infatuations. We crave comfort, success and prestige. We work for more money, greater influence and power. We lust for fame and sexual gratification. 'If only I had that job, had a better sex life, had a sex life, was married, was divorced, ate less, ate more, was taller, shorter, thinner, more muscular, had a faster car, a bigger house–then I would be truly satisfied.'

But the objects of our desire elude us.

What's more, as the Catholic spiritual writer Ronald Rolheiser says, we will only find release when we recognise that our desire not only eludes us but deludes us as well. It is vital that we come to accept this 'because it is only then that we will stop demanding that life–our partners, our families, our friends, our jobs, our vocations and vacations–give us something that they cannot give, namely the finished symphony, clear-cut, pure joy, complete consummation'.[3]

There was once a man who spotted a beautiful star in the sky and longed to visit it. He became obsessed with reaching that glistening star and so decided to set about building a rocket to take him there. He cut down trees and dug up coal. His factories burnt fuel and spewed out smoke. The man didn't care how much rubbish was churned out or how much waste mounted up, as long as he could build himself a rocket to visit that star.

At last the day came when the rocket was ready. So the man went to the tallest mountain of waste and blasted off towards the star he so longed to see. But, having travelled for many months, when he arrived on the star there was nothing. It was barren, stark, cold and bare. The only thing to look at was another star, far, far away. It glistened and beckoned as it shone more brightly and beautifully than any sight he had ever seen in the dark sky. So the man decided to visit that star instead.

Meanwhile, those left behind on Earth decided that the roads and the rubbish, the factories and fumes and filth, had to go. They set about getting rid of the man's legacy of waste. Plants began to bloom again, flowers flourished once more, and the Earth was renewed.

As the man travelled towards his new star, he had no idea that it was the Earth he had left behind so long ago. And when he first got there he simply didn't recognise it. He was sure that it was paradise. Until at last it became clear to him: this was the beautiful star he had never appreciated in the first place and which he had almost destroyed in his longing to get somewhere else."

Longing is an emotion we learn young. Children are often preoccupied with wanting a new toy, a new fun adventure, more freedom, more independence. And, as teenagers, we hunger to plunge ourselves into the delights of adulthood.

As the French proverb has it: 'The first half of life is spent in longing for the second–the second half in regretting the first.'

A young boy wants a horse.
The boy is given a horse for his fourteenth birthday.
The apprentice says, 'How wonderful.'
The teacher says, 'We'll see.'
The boy falls off his horse and breaks his leg.
The apprentice says, 'How terrible.'
The teacher says, 'We'll see.'
A war breaks out but the boy does not have to go to fight because his leg is broken.
The apprentice says, 'How wonderful.'
The teacher says, 'We'll see . . .'[5]

Many–though sadly not all–of us have the privilege of spending childhood like seagoing yachts in the safety of a harbour, protected from the raging elements. Storms may pound and crash against those harbour walls, but our parents, our family and our communities are there to rally round, keeping the worst of it at bay. However, as we grow, despite an increased awareness of the trials and tribulations that may await us, a longing to set sail is awakened, a longing to leave the shelter of the harbour walls behind us and take our chances on the high seas of life in search of the promise of far-flung lands and their treasures.

The world is our oyster, we are told–and oysters sometimes contain pearls. We are intrigued by the possibility of hidden treasures. There are so many experiences to be had, so much to discover. Life is a party and we have been invited. We are desperate to touch and taste the goodies on offer without restriction or restraint.

HAPPINESS MACHINES

And soon, beyond these early longings, arrives another set of desires–deeper than the first–the desire to acquire.

Yet how many of us find that as soon as we've acquired something we thought we really needed, we simply start craving something else?

We are, in the words of Ed Bernays (the nephew of Freud and the man who in the 1920s gave to the world the science of public relations), 'happiness machines'. But our happiness levels are driven by irrational emotions, unconscious cravings, submerged desires and unrecognised longings for fulfilment. Our desires overshadow our needs.

Human desire drives us into the arms of the god of the new age–consumerism.

As consumers, we are seduced more by the *desire* to acquire than by the *possession* of the object itself. We find more pleasure in the chase than in the ownership, with which we become easily bored. Whether it's a car, a house, a dress or a gadget, it is the power and experience of buying, not the resulting ownership, to which the consumer is so often addicted.

Thus, we are never satisfied. We may have the house, the car, the plasma widescreen telly with surround sound, the espresso coffeemaker, and the sit-on lawnmower–but there's always that yacht in the marina.

Richard, in Alex Garland's *The Beach*, says, 'Mine is a generation that circles the globe in search of something we haven't tried before.'[6]

For many, shopping is the highest high we can get that's legal. Accumulation has become the road to Utopia–acquiring the right car, the right clothes, the right coffee, the right PDA, even the right toilet paper–perfect. Well, perfect until tomorrow's magazine introduces us to the next upgrade, the new model or the freshest design. We consume without guilt or shame and happily display our purchased identity via the universal language of the logo, thus revealing our commitment to the West's dominant philosophy, *Consumo, ergo sum*–I shop, therefore I am.

In 1985, the American sociologist Neil Postman published what would become an influential, best-selling book, *Amusing Ourselves to Death*. In this book he compared and contrasted two different visions of the future: the vision set out by George Orwell, in his novel *1984* (published in 1949), and the vision of Aldous Huxley, in his novel *Brave New World* (written in 1931).

Orwell feared we would be overcome by externally imposed oppression (in the form of 'Big Brother,' the all-seeing eye that watches everybody's every move), but Huxley saw that people would come to choose their own self-imposed oppression through their addiction to technologies that destroy their ability to think.

Orwell feared that the authorities would ban books, but Huxley worried that there would be no reason to ban books–no one would want to read them.

Orwell feared those who would deprive us of information, but Huxley worried about those who would provide us with so much information that we would be reduced to passivity.

Orwell believed that truth would be concealed from us, but Huxley feared that truth would be lost in our self-made sea of irrelevance.

Orwell feared that we would become a captive culture, but Huxley feared that we would become a trivial culture.

Orwell feared that what we hate will ruin us, but Huxley saw that what we love will ruin us; Western societies would dance themselves into oblivion, suffocated in their own trivia. In Orwell's writing people are controlled by having pain inflicted on them. In Huxley's picture of the future, they are controlled by self-induced pleasure.

Surely it was Huxley who read the signs of the times more accurately.

Some years ago I talked to a television cameraman who had just returned from South America. He told me the tale of how, while he was there, he had visited a remote rural community, and how shocked he was by the misery he saw there.

I asked him what had caused the suffering–was it a lack of water, food, work, health?

'No,' he said, 'it was caused by the building of a road.'

I looked puzzled.

He said, 'I first visited the village five years ago. Life there was idyllic. There was little or no crime. Family and community life was strong. The young respected and honoured the old. The people were happy. But back in those days, it took me the best part of a day to travel across the pothole-ridden dirt track to get there. However, the visit I've just made was very different. At some point over the last five years, they put in a concrete road. And the road has brought trade and electricity and TVs and fashion – and showed the people all the things that they did not have. And now the community is as rife with crime and depression and unhappiness and jealousy as anywhere else. The road ruined the village.'

Driven by advertising and the media of television, radio and the Internet, we find ourselves titillated and over-stimulated in our restlessness. Yet we still believe the lie that somewhere 'out there' others have found something we haven't. That their lives are somehow more fulfilling, more complete than ours. That our lives are too small. So we go in search of back-to-back experiences to meet our needs or, at the very least, fill the emptiness.

FREEDOM THROUGH DISCIPLINE

Ironically, even as our culture intensifies and trivialises our desires, we all know that real happiness isn't found at the end of a till queue. Possessions don't buy us happiness, just a numbing of the pain. Perhaps all the more surprising is that we have come to find that living without boundaries is not the route to happiness either.

Becoming an apprentice of Jesus Christ begins by discovering that discipline is the friend of freedom, not its enemy. Astonishing as it may at first seem, discipline is actually the pathway to the fulfilment of our deep longings and desires.

As Esther de Waal reflects, 'I know only too well from my own experience that a life without boundaries can never become a life that is constructive, creative and life-giving.'[7]

In the English-speaking world, the word *discipline* often gets muddled, confused with the concepts of 'punishment' and 'restriction' rather than being associated with training and freedom. Often, when a parent speaks of 'disciplining' their child, we automatically assume they have told them off, grounded them ... or worse still.

Even *The Oxford Pocket Dictionary of Current English* has, as its first definition of the word *discipline*, 'the practice of training people to obey rules or a code of behaviour, using punishment to correct disobedience.'[8]

However, strange as it may seem, we find that discipline, rather than curtailing, freedom, is an essential part of every apprentice's journey towards it. Rather than being a punishment, discipline is a means of enhancing and enriching our journey. This is evident from the very etymology of the word: *discipline* is derived from the Latin *disciplina*, meaning 'instruction given to a disciple'.

Every week the boy would walk the two miles to the home of his piano teacher, clutching his small pile of sheet music, ready for his hour-long lesson. He would dutifully listen to the instruction given him and look as interested as he could. He would then do his best to perform as required and enthusiastically agree to practise his scales, do his sight-reading and learn the set pieces for the following week. But the truth is, he hated his piano lessons. It wasn't that he didn't want to be able to play. Ever since he had seen Freddie Mercury from Queen pound out the classic anthem 'Bohemian Rhapsody', he had dreamed of playing in a band, touring the world, taking the applause of adoring fans and living the life of a rich and famous rock star. The problem was he couldn't understand why he had to waste his time playing the tunes of nursery rhymes and practising scales and arpeggios when he wanted to be playing the rock songs he loved.

For month after month he went, but progress was painfully slow. He never practised between lessons. He felt trapped. This wasn't how it was meant to be. Where was the excitement and the pleasure that he had witnessed on the faces of the performers he watched on TV?

His teacher had been as patient as she could be with him. But then, after a particularly unenthusiastic attempt at playing the set piece, the boy's teacher exploded.

'You're wasting my time and yours! You turn up here every week, hand over your parents' hard-earned money and pretend to be interested in playing the piano. But the reality is, you never practise. By now you should be at least grade three, but you haven't even reached the standard necessary to take your first grade. I know it can feel frustrating that we don't always play the things you would like, but you can't run before you can walk. If you think you are ever going to be able to play the piano by daydreaming instead of practising, then you can think again.'

The boy was completely taken aback. That night he told his parents what had happened, and he never went to a piano lesson again.

That was over twenty years ago. Sometimes, when he is alone, the man now sits at the piano he has in his house and picks over the keys. His wife plays very well and his daughter often performs recitals at her school, but the man doesn't even have the confidence or the skills to play in front of his own family. His dreams of playing in a band have long passed. He still admires other pianists, how their hands glide over the keys, the freedom with which they express themselves. As a child he thought freedom was expressed in not being disciplined or committed to practising. Now he lives with regret and the knowledge that he wished he had learned earlier–discipline is the pathway to freedom.

The failure to discipline our desires will often bring us to a place of regret. Longing and regret frequently go hand in hand. It's a lose-lose situation. If we acquire what we long for, we often simply start craving something else. If we fail to acquire it, we waste our energy in regret.

THE INNER JOURNEY

Carl Jung, the famous Swiss psychiatrist, believed that the second half of life gives us a new opportunity for spiritual development. It is the period of life when the 'external' quest for prosperity and status begins to be superseded by the 'internal' search for meaning and fulfilment as we learn to reflect, more deeply, on the purpose of life. He wrote:

> We cannot live the afternoon of life according to the programme of life's morning; for what was great in the morning will be little at evening, and what in the morning was true will at evening have become a lie.[9]

Jung believed that life's middle years (the afternoon of life), like old age (the evening) and youth (the morning), all play specific roles in our spiritual development. While youth is about turning outwards, the goal for the second half of life is to give attention to the inner journey. Avoiding this inner journey often leaves us in a state of depression as we struggle with an absence of meaning in our lives. In the afternoon and evening of our lives, we must choose to move beyond the external concerns of our younger years. If we ignore our inner voice and take refuge in the continued accumulation of things, we experience a form of living death, the deterioration of our soul. In the same essay, 'The Stages of Life,' Jung wrote:

> Among all my patients in the second half of life–that is to say, over 35 years–there has not been one whose problem in the last resort was not finding a religious outlook on life ... and none of them has been really healed who did not regain his religious outlook.[10]

The Bible never denies the power of longing. Rather, it contains numerous stories and sayings about it:

> *All my longings lie open before you, O Lord;*
> *my sighing is not hidden from you.*
>
> Psalm 38:9

> *You listen to the longings of those who suffer.*
> *You offer them hope, and you pay attention to*
> *their cries for help.*
>
> Psalm 10:17 CEV

Our longings and desires are often used by God to move us forward in our journey. As M. Scott Peck has said, 'The truth is that our finest moments are most likely to occur when we are feeling deeply uncomfortable, unhappy, or unfulfilled. For it is only in such moments, propelled by our discomfort, that we are likely to step out of our ruts and start searching for different ways or truer answers.'[11] Deep desires motivate us to seek answers. In our most desperate moments, we are called to look outside of ourselves.

LONGING FOR GOD

Among the many things they learned from their rabbi, the apprentices of Jesus were taught how to pray. In his most famous prayer, in Matthew 6:9–15, Jesus urged his apprentices to focus their longings towards God in a way that would make a real difference in the world–today.

> *Our Father in heaven,*
> *hallowed be your name,*
> *your kingdom come,*
> *your will be done*
> *on earth as it is in heaven.*
> *Give us today our daily bread.*
> *Forgive us our debts,*
> *as we also have forgiven our debtors.*
> *And lead us not into temptation,*
> *but deliver us from the evil one.*
> *For if you forgive men when they sin against you, your heavenly Father will also forgive you. But if you do not forgive men their sins, your Father will not forgive your sins.*

For many, this prayer may be so familiar that it has become almost banal. In reality, however, it is a prayer that expresses deep longing and desire: longing for the ushering in of God's kingdom on earth; desire that God's hopes for us will come to fruition, here and now.

When we are young we are told to 'say' our prayers. But prayers are not primarily words that are 'said'. Real prayer is a longing, a yearning, an aching that will not go away. An apprentice's prayer is an ongoing approach to life that says, for all my inconsistencies and failings, this is my passion, this is my deepest desire. This is why I am here, my purpose in life. This is who I am.

Reflecting on this longing, Dietrich Bonhoeffer wrote:

> The longing for God that consumes the soul is true for all times. It cannot be otherwise when it comes from God himself. It must be forever. It has practically nothing to do with an emotional surge or single dedication of the heart to God's Word. It is a decision made for all time.[12]

Prayer is more than just asking. It is a longing. We may, from time to time, use words to express the true longings of our heart. But when we pray, it is always better to have a heart without words than to have words without a heart.

LONGING FOR JUSTICE

Jesus showed us that if we channel our longing into questions about life, justice, fighting for the truth, speaking up for those who lack a voice, liberating those trapped in poverty, befriending the forgotten–then our passion has meaning and purpose.

And if through our apprenticeship to Christ we begin to long not for material gain for ourselves but for everyone to be fed, clothed and loved, then our longing becomes fruitful. Because when we really start longing for justice, action follows.

This kind of longing is painful. It hurts. It is an aching that never leaves us. But it is out of the very process of this constant yearning that change slowly comes. Because longing is a great motivator. As Albert Einstein once said, 'Feeling and longing are the motive forces behind all human endeavour and human creations.'[13]

Paul, a first-century apprentice of Christ, writes about this kind of longing to his friends in the city of Corinth, in 2 Corinthians 7:11. He acknowledges that longing and sorrow go hand in hand, but he also reminds them that the fruit of this sorrow is something real and tangible: a desire to get things done.

> See what this godly sorrow has produced in you: what earnestness, what eagerness ... what indignation, what alarm, what longing, what concern, what readiness to see justice done.

Perhaps the key to apprenticeship is not simply to ask God to bless our desires, but to align our longings with the desires of God. What if life is really about discovering what God is up to and joining in?

Jesus said: 'Do not work for the food that spoils, but work for the food that will never spoil, the food that will give you life for ever' (John 6:27 WE).[14]

'"My food," said Jesus, "is to do the will of him who sent me and to finish his work"' (John 4:34).

This is a strange comment. We are conditioned to think of work as exhausting and draining, even as de-humanising. But Jesus makes an extraordinary statement. He presents his work–doing the will of God–as his food. Food is life-giving. It nourishes us. It energises us.

Thus, if our longings are channelled into the kind of work Jesus was talking about, our desires no longer drain us–they sustain us.

Our yearning becomes the motivation to do God's work: that 'readiness to see justice done' that Paul wrote about, and the energy to put those words into action.

Now that's a pathway worth pursuing!

3

BELIEVING

The tube train was packed as it trundled through central London. Most people were going about their business, oblivious to their travelling companions, but one young man had become preoccupied with the rather perplexed and obviously disoriented elderly gentleman who sat opposite him.

The elderly man kept looking down at a map of the Underground in the front of his diary, then up at the maps displayed in the train and out of the window as the train passed through each station in turn. From time to time he'd scratch his head and sigh.

Eventually the young man decided to go against the tube's usual social code, approach the elderly gentleman and offer his assistance. Immediately his instincts were confirmed; this man was not English–he was Eastern-European and on his first trip to the UK. Taking the diary that contained the map, the young man stared at it, determined to locate exactly where they were. He didn't travel on the Underground very often, so he was no expert. Turning the diary one way and then the other, he couldn't make head nor tail of it either. Finally, in frustration, he gave up and closed it–and that's when he understood.

The diary was French. The map inside its cover wasn't of the London tube at all–it was the Paris Metro!

We all exercise trust every day. Everyone. Bar none. We have to. We drive cars someone else designed, we eat meals someone else prepared, we enter elevators someone else serviced. And, whether well-placed or misguided, whether intentional or subconscious, trust is a behaviour we all recognise as natural.

In other words, everyone lives by faith. There is no other option. Whether we place our faith in science, religion, education, government, the justice system–or nothing more than the accuracy of the tube map in the front of our diary–each one of us lives by faith in whatever we trust to be reliable and true.

LIVING BY FAITH

Our reason, past experience, emotions, friends and families, culture–all these combine to help determine who or what it is that we trust. The decisions we make each day reveal what we hold to be true. I trust that my car will get me to work, that my bank will keep my money safe, that my vote will be counted and that the government I vote for will deliver on its promises. I put faith into action every day of my life.

There is a widespread myth that faith is the exclusive possession of those who hold religious beliefs. But this is false. In fact, it turns out that the statements 'I believe in God' and 'I don't believe in God' are, equally, statements of faith.

The difference between believing that God exists and believing that God does *not* exist is not the difference between the 'presence' and 'absence' of faith–it is simply a difference in the *content* of that faith and belief. Indeed, just as the world is filled with self-appointed salesmen for God, it is also filled with evangelical atheists who are equally determined to convert anyone who will listen to their belief system, their faith in the non-existence of God.

People often talk about the 'presence' or 'absence' of faith as though it's something we either have or don't have, as though it's either here or gone, as though it could be held in our hands or could slip through our fingers.

But faith is more dynamic than that. If we imagine faith to be something concrete and permanent, we miss the point. Once we recognise that faith is something we *all* exercise–to one degree or another–then any struggle is not about whether we *can* believe but about *what*–or *whom*–we choose to believe and how deeply we feel that trust.

The real question, then, is not 'do you have faith?' Rather, are the people, the organisations, the investments, the promises and the relationships you put your faith in day by day, year by year, really worth your investment of trust?

Years ago I sat and watched a TV programme in which experts put forward the following hypothesis: our brains are wired to believe in God. Tiny electrical impulses around the temporal lobe area induce in us a sense of the transcendent. For some there is a stronger awareness than for others, but we all have it. Some of the research scientists on the programme argued that this is a survival mechanism that helps the human race cope with trauma, such as death. It helps us to move on from painful experiences in the belief that, ultimately, we will be taken care of by a higher being. It gives us a common story, a core set of beliefs that holds us together.

Some may conclude from this that God is nothing more than a product of our evolutionary development, an electrical impulse in our brains. But this is missing the point. As one of the scientists involved concluded, this research needn't lead us to the assumption that God doesn't exist. The evidence can only demonstrate that this 'wiring' is in our brains. For all we know this could be the way God has made us so that we can connect to him.

And so, all our scientific research brings us right back to the core question.

The question of faith.

THE BIGGER PICTURE

> He who has a why can endure any how.[1]

Without a *why* we are lost. Writing about this problem in his book *The Gay Science*, Nietzsche described an age that believed it no longer needed God:

> *Do we hear the noise of the grave-diggers*
> *who are burying God?*
> *Do we not smell the divine putrefaction?–for*
> *even Gods putrefy!*
> *God is dead!*
> *God remains dead!*
> *And we have killed him!*
> *How shall we console ourselves,*
> *the most murderous of all murderers?...*
> *Is not the magnitude of this deed too great*
> *for us?*
> *Shall we not ourselves have to become gods,*
> *merely to seem worthy of it?*[2]

Nietzsche's 'God is dead' statement has become one of the most widely quoted and deeply misunderstood phrases of the last hundred years. But in *Thus Spake Zarathustra*, he predicted what he feared would be the outcome of the death or, as he called it, the 'murder' of God. He believed that secular people, having lost touch with transcendence, would also lose any reference point from which to steer their lives or judge themselves.[3]

Nietzsche's contemporary, the Christian writer and philosopher Fyodor Dostoyevsky, explored the same themes in his books *Brothers Karamazov* and *The Idiot*, concluding that if we cease to believe in God, there can be no morality, for 'without God everything is permitted' and all values are meaningless.[4]

Once the authority of God is removed, then every man and woman becomes their own ultimate source of authority. The *why* of life–that sense of meaning and purpose that guides our moral convictions–is lost. The result is a chaotic and damaging culture in which each person puts his or her own interests first, to the detriment of the whole of society.

On 30 April 1999, at the height of the NATO bombing of Serbia, the president of the Czech Republic, Václav Havel, addressed both houses of the Canadian Parliament. Havel used his speech to express his deep conviction that the greatest political challenge of the twenty-first century will be to ensure that all nation-states submit to the rule of international law and uphold universal human rights. He concluded with these words:

> I have often asked myself why human beings have any rights at all. I have always come to the conclusion that human rights, human freedoms, and human dignity have their deepest roots somewhere outside the perceptible world. These values ... make sense only in the perspective of the infinite and the eternal ... Allow me to conclude my remarks on the state and its probable role in future with the assertion that, while the state is a human creation, human beings are the creation of God.[5]

MADE IN THE IMAGE OF GOD

On its first page, in the first chapter of the first book, the Bible explains that humanity is made in the 'image of God' (Genesis 1:27). But what does this actually mean? Since the Bible teaches us that God is spirit, we know that it isn't referring to a physical resemblance. Our 'God-likeness' must, therefore, be found in the fact that we, too, are spiritual beings.

But reading the creation account in Genesis 1 reveals something more. While the rest of creation is physical and material, God only chooses to breathe his Spirit into human beings.

This means that people have a unique place in creation. Every human being is stamped with the image of the Creator. Human life is more than a biological reality. Each one of us is a fusion of the physical and spiritual.

And although some persist in preaching that belief in God is a 'primitive' idea which we need to shed, many are still striving to find ways of connecting with their innate sense that we are, in our very essence, more than just flesh and blood. There is an indefinable aspect of our human psyche that longs for the 'spiritual'. And it's this spiritual instinct that takes us forward on our quest for purpose, meaning and fulfilment.

According to Genesis, we are neither physical bodies with a spiritual side, nor spiritual beings somehow trapped in physical bodies. In our very formation, we represent the full integration of the physical with the spiritual. Therefore, when we stand before another person, whoever they are–however destitute, disabled, diseased or degraded–we stand before a vehicle of the divine.

French biologist Jean Rostand puts it this way: 'For my part I believe there is no life that … does not deserve respect and is not worth defending with zeal and conviction … I would almost measure society's degree of civilization by the amount of effort and vigilance it imposes on itself out of pure respect for life.'[6]

Throughout church history, Christian writers have universally believed that the 'image of God' (or *imago Dei*,[7] as they have called it) remains present whether or not a person chooses to acknowledge God. The 'image of God' is precisely what constitutes our intrinsic value and worth as human beings and, therefore, it cannot be lost. The famous fifth-century church leader Augustine taught that in each human being, 'although worn out and defaced by losing the participation of God, yet the image of God still remains'.

Each and every person, however far they have wandered from God, continues to bear the imprint of God in their life. This means that every person, regardless of their background, has the capacity to become an apprentice of Christ–and, by extension, an apprentice of the God in whose image we are made.

Recognising that we are all made in God's image means recognising another truth: we are all, like God, spiritual beings.

HEALTHY SPIRITUALITY

So, when people make comments like 'I am a spiritual person,' they are right. They may not be a Christian, a member of another faith, or even believe in God, but they have still grasped a deep truth. Even the World Health Organization recognises that 'Human Flourishing' and well-being include spiritual health. Ignoring or denying the spiritual aspect of our human condition is a dead-end. In order to thrive we must acknowledge that we are, indeed, spiritual beings.

And, while we are all spiritual beings, we must not forget that we are also consumers: a problematic combination!

If you type 'spirituality' into an Internet search engine, you'll find yourself bombarded by thousands of possible spiritualities to sample. From the major world religions to paganism, Jainism or horoscopes, we find a fashionably eclectic and often exotic cut-and-paste approach to spirituality.

Spirituality is now a consumer choice, and, it seems, the customer is always right. For many today, it no longer matters *what* you believe–whether it's bespoke or off-the-shelf spirituality–because almost every spirituality is viewed as equally valid.

Junk spirituality, it seems, is every bit as prevalent as junk food. But only the foolish believe something just because a so-called wise person told them to, or because a belief is generally held or is considered to be fashionable. We should never believe something just because someone else believes it. Take time to consider what is really worthwhile, what is essential. Which beliefs will enrich your life *and* those of the people around you, and which are fundamentally based on self-interest?

> A simple man believes anything,
> but a prudent man gives thought to his
> steps.
>
> Proverbs 14:15

Even as we stop to consider our beliefs, we must bear in mind the distinction between *thinking* about our beliefs and making an *act* of faith. Whatever we choose to believe, we must always recognise that our knowledge is limited, partial, incomplete. Whether we believe in astronomy or astrology, religion or reason, philosophy or fact, ultimately we have to exercise trust.

John Kavanaugh, a brilliant ethicist, went to live for three months in Mother Teresa's 'House of the Dying' in Calcutta on a personal pilgrimage to find guidance and a clear vision for the rest of his life.

On his very first morning, Mother Teresa asked Kavanaugh, as she asked everyone, 'What can I do for you?' He requested that she pray for him. So she asked him what, specifically, he would like her to pray about.

Without hesitation, Kavanaugh, who had travelled thousands of miles on his quest, replied, 'Please pray that I get clarity for the future.'

'No!' retorted Mother Teresa emphatically, 'I will not do that . . . Clarity is the last thing you are clinging to and must let go of.'

'But you always seem to have clarity,' Kavanaugh spluttered, a little taken aback. With a twinkle in her eye, Mother Teresa laughed. 'I have never had clarity; but what I have always had is trust. So I will pray that you trust God.'[8]

LISTENING FOR GOD

God is subtle. God is not in your face the whole time; which is why it is possible for many of us to get by in life without recognising or acknowledging him.

God grants freedom to each one of us. For him it is enough to paint the multi-coloured rainbow in the blue sky, the green grass on the rich dark soil, the hazy beauty of the rolling hills, the rugged grandeur of the mountain face. He does not feel the need to manipulate cloud formations in such a way as to spell out Bible verses in giant letters or give us warnings of eternal peril and judgment. God does not bully or threaten us into believing. He does not make things so factually undeniable that no faith is necessary on our part.

God has the kind of relaxed, gentle attitude which, unfortunately, is not shared by many of the people who act as his self-appointed agents.

God leaves us the space to make our own decisions and choices. He leaves his door open, but it is up to us whether or not we venture through.

An apprentice dropped his gold ring inside his house. But the house was dark and there was a great amount of furniture which he needed to move in order to continue his search. So, lacking the determination his task required, he went outside and began to look around the courtyard.

His teacher passed by and asked him what he was looking for.

'I have lost my gold ring,' said the apprentice.

'Where did you lose it?' asked his teacher.

'In my bedroom,' said the apprentice.

'Then why are you looking for it out here?'

'There's more room out here,' the apprentice replied. 'It makes my task easier.'

If we have lost something as valuable as our sense of meaning or purpose, then looking for it in the place where we lost it–rather than searching within our comfort zones–will make all the difference. French essayist and novelist Marcel Proust is widely credited with the following observation:

> The real voyage of discovery consists not in seeking new lands, but seeing with new eyes.[9]

And if you want to find God, you have to look for him. God will not force himself on you. Contrary to popular belief, God *invites* us into a relationship with him. His is a loving request, not an intimidating threat. God gently woos us. God comes to embrace, not to bully. God is a lover, not a rapist.

Two men, deep in conversation, walked down a bustling city street. One is at home, the other is visiting from the country-side.

Passing a tree, the visitor suddenly stopped. 'Can you hear that?' he asked as pedestrians squeezed and bumped past them.

'Hear what?' his friend replied.

'The cricket singing. It must be in the tree.' He leant with one ear leaning towards the tree to tune into the source of the song.

'There's no cricket, it's in your head!' the city worker exclaimed, as a woman walked by shouting into her phone. 'And, even if there were, you'd never be able to hear it over the noise of all these people and this traffic.'

The visitor's friend laughed and walked on.

But, as he did so, the visitor pulled a small coin from his pocket and let it drop to the ground. The coin hit the pavement and quietly rolled to a rest.

Intuitively his friend twisted his head round, glancing over his shoulder at the ground to search for the coin. At the same moment, perhaps twenty other pedestrians surreptitiously scanned the ground as they walked by.

With a smile, the visitor looked at his friend and said, 'You're listening to the wrong tune.'

When we become attuned to the music of creation, we notice God's harmonies everywhere. We hear them in the echoes of the mountain range and the heaving of the sea, sitting round a meal table with friends, in the shining eyes of an old man who allows a memory to touch the surface of his mind, in the quiet contentment of a babbling baby.

Those who do not listen will not hear. Those who do not search will see nothing but the obvious: 'in spite of his wonders, they did not believe,' writes the psalmist–the great lyricist of the Bible–in Psalm 78:32.

An apprentice, coming in from the bright sunlight, entered a dark room at great speed–he was in a hurry and wanted to be elsewhere.

He had been told that the room was filled with priceless treasure and so, although cynical, he wanted to check for himself, just in case, before dismissing the claims.

He glanced quickly around the room and, just as he suspected, he could see absolutely nothing except the darkness.

So he turned on his heel and left, happy that he had proved himself right.

If at first you see nothing, stay awhile, reflect awhile, and let your eyes adjust. A whole new world may open up to you. Only when we stop, linger and wait until our eyes readjust from the distractions and desires that fill our lives, can we begin to see what has always been there.

'Help me to find God,' said the apprentice.

'No one can help you there,' said his teacher.

'Why not?' enquired the apprentice.

'For the same reason that no one can help the fish to find the ocean.'[10]

Jim Wallis, a self-confessed activist, puts it this way:

> Contemplation may be the most difficult thing for activists, yet it may be the most important thing. Action without reflection can easily become barren and bitter. Without the space for self-examination and the capacity for rejuvenation, the danger of exhaustion and despair is too great. And at an even deeper level, contemplation confronts us with the questions of our identity and power. Who are we? To whom do we belong? Is there a power that is greater than ours? How can we know it? Contemplation can be a frightening thing.[11]

While it can be frightening to examine our lives in this way, it is through contemplation that we allow ourselves time to reflect on which beliefs we hold dear–and whether they are truly worthwhile. It is through contemplation that we can take time out from the cynicism of our culture and start to renew our sense of trust. Trust is an integral part of apprenticeship; if we choose to trust Jesus, then we choose to follow him – we choose to be his apprentices.

Nearly eight hundred years before the time of Jesus, a sage by the name of Isaiah spoke of the kind of trust that God invites us to place in him:

> *Fear not, for I have redeemed you;*
> *I have summoned you by name; you are mine.*
> *When you pass through the waters,*
> *I will be with you;*
> *and when you pass through the rivers,*
> *they will not sweep over you.*
> *When you walk through the fire,*
> *you will not be burned;*
> *the flames will not set you ablaze.*
> *For I am the LORD, your God.*
>
> Isaiah 43:1 – 3

In the end, choosing to follow Christ, to become his apprentice, is an act of faith. It involves believing; it's an act of letting go. And this faith will always be mysterious and uncontainable – for the simple reason that God himself is these things.

The apprentice was worried; he was full of questions about God's nature.

The teacher smiled. 'God is a wonderful paradox: known yet unknowable, explicable yet inexplicable, visible yet invisible. Every statement I make about him, every answer to your questions, therefore, can only be a partial truth.'

The apprentice was bewildered. 'Then why do you speak about him at all?'

'Why does the bird sing?' said the teacher. 'Because it has a song.'[12]

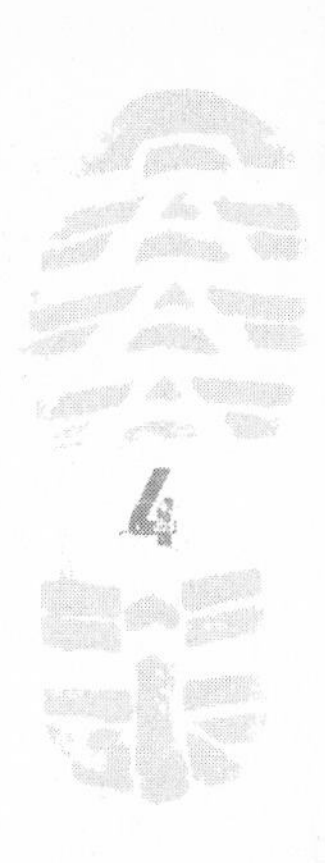

4 QUESTIONING

A young man tells his brother of a dream he's experienced, a dream about Jesus returning. Not in the 'Second Coming', but on a visit to sixteenth-century Seville, when the Spanish Inquisition was at the height of its powers.

No fanfare greets Jesus' return; instead he walks to Seville Cathedral, where he is arrested by the Cardinal Grand Inquisitor. The Inquisitor visits him in prison, informing him that he'll be burnt at the stake the following day. He remains silent as the Inquisitor explains: Jesus will be put to death because he jeopardises people's salvation. He gives them too much freedom.

Although everyone is born with freedom, the Inquisitor argues, only a select few have the moral integrity to handle determining right from wrong. Only the elite can be trusted to face doubt and uncertainty and come through with their beliefs intact. Most people just can't cope.

'I tell you,' the Grand Inquisitor continues, 'humans are pathetic creatures, with no more urgent need than to find someone to whom they can surrender the gift of freedom they were born with.' This was the point that Jesus failed to grasp the first time, he claims. By refusing to demonstrate his power in the wilderness or come down from the cross–actions that would have proved his identity and power beyond all doubt–he saddled people with the crippling burden of having to think for themselves.

'We've corrected your mighty achievement,' the old man boasts, defending the brutal way in which the Inquisition forced people to believe the Church's doctrines.

'People will accept whatever we tell them with joy because they have been spared the anguish and torment of having to make their own free and independent choices.'[1]

God gives us freedom of choice. He doesn't coerce or manoeuvre us into believing in him. He doesn't give us an 'offer we can't refuse'. And so it is that our questions are never to be feared. Indeed, what is far more worrying is a culture in which people either don't have any questions or, still worse, do not feel free to raise them.

The very nature of faith implies uncertainty. Without room for doubt, faith could not exist. Our only remaining option would

yearn for more signs, more certainty. Doubts, it seems, are always with us. Actor and director Woody Allen summed it up this way:

> If only God would give me some clear sign! Like making a large deposit in my name at a Swiss bank.[5]

Tony Burke, an atheist who worked in the porn industry, was looking for a sign, some evidence of God, when he embarked on his journey for the UK television series *The Monastery* (Tiger Aspect Productions, Ltd./BBC). Tony's experiences were fascinating. For a number of weeks, Tony and several other volunteers became residents of an English Benedictine monastery, Worth Abbey, where their experiences were filmed. During a mentoring session with one of the monks there, the change in Tony's perception was palpable. As an audience of millions watched – many of whom strongly identified with Tony and warmed to his honesty – his doubts visibly dissolved. Afterwards, Tony recorded in his video diary that:

> 'I didn't want this to happen ... When I woke up this morning, I didn't believe in this, but, as I speak to you now, I do.'[6]

Tony encountered God by allowing enough time, space and silence to explore his questions about faith – and to listen for a response.

How many of us, with our hectic schedules, are able to give ourselves the time, space and silence to let our doubts breathe? For many, the big questions of life slowly eat away at us, unresolved, while we spend our time, day in, day out, dealing with the smaller but more pressing issues that grab our attention.

We like certainty. We like things to be beyond doubt–black and white, on or off, right or wrong. We dislike ambiguity. We prefer things to be cut and dried and guaranteed. We don't want to spend our days agonizing over life's difficult questions. Yet, ironically, one of the few things we *can* be absolutely certain of is that God doesn't supply that kind of certainty.

PROBE YOUR DOUBTS

> There are two ways to slide easily through life: to believe everything or to doubt everything; both ways save us from thinking.
>
> Alfred Korzybski (1879–1950)

Christ invited, but never compelled, his apprentices to exercise faith. He refused to do things that would *force* people into trusting him. He left room for his followers to doubt him and encouraged them to explore those doubts. Yet he also challenged their assumptions, raising questions that would, ultimately, deepen their faith in him.

When one of his first apprentices had doubts about his resurrection from the dead, Jesus didn't force the issue. Rather than reprimanding Thomas for his doubts, Jesus invited him to acknowledge them and to take action by engaging with them. 'Put your finger here and look at my hands! Put your hand into my side. Stop doubting and have faith!' (John 20:27 CEV).

Today, separated from the original event by two thousand years, it's easy for us to misread the tone of this encounter. We view the story through a succession of cultural filters that impair our vision. We are tempted – even taught – to hear in Jesus' words a tone of impatience and frustration – of demand rather than gentle invitation. However, it's worth noticing that Jesus encourages Thomas to turn from his doubt only *after* the invitation and opportunity to explore those doubts. Jesus invites Thomas to investigate his questions (literally putting his hands into the wounds of Jesus) with the kind of in-depth probing most of us would find shocking.

As far as we can ascertain from the story, Thomas never did take Jesus up on his offer. Jesus was prepared to give Thomas far more space than he needed to face his questions, and in the end Thomas didn't feel the need to explore his doubts any further: because the simple invitation to do so freed him from them. A sharp rebuke might have pulled Thomas into line, but the invitation to explore his questions ultimately enabled him to deepen his faith in Jesus.

Thomas might have been slower than his fellow apprentices to develop faith in the risen Christ, but when he did so, that faith was expressed in language which went beyond any that they had found: 'My Lord and my God!' (John 20:28).

> He who asks a question is a fool for five minutes; he who does not ask a question remains a fool forever.
>
> Chinese Proverb

Paradoxically, doubt isn't the opposite of faith; it sits near the heart of it. Faith and doubt are inextricably linked. Doubt is always a part of the journey of faith. We see this paradox in the words of the man who brought his sick son to Jesus seeking healing: 'I do believe; help me overcome my unbelief!' (Mark 9:24). In the words of Cardinal Basil Hume: 'Doubt is the instrument to purify my faith. It is only when I begin to doubt that I really make an honest act of faith.'[7] Naquib Mahfouz added this: 'You can tell whether a man is clever by his answers. You can tell whether a man is wise by his questions.'[8]

Our beliefs should not come from a rejection of reason, but rather from the honest outcome of an ongoing debate in which we use our reason to probe our faith. As David Bowie put it: 'Just because I believe don't mean I don't think as well.'[9]

A man left his brand-new bicycle unattended in a crowded marketplace while he went about his shopping.

Some hours later he remembered that he had forgotten to lock it. He rushed to the place where he had left it, expecting to find that it had been stolen.

To his surprise, the bicycle was exactly where he had left it.

Overwhelmed with joy, he rode it to the nearby church to thank God for having kept his bicycle safe.

But when he got out of the church, the bicycle was gone.

Growing in faith teaches us to expect the unexpected, to look beneath the surface of life and ask the questions no one else is asking. As philosopher Francis Bacon said: 'If a man will begin with certainties, he shall end in doubts. But if he will be content to begin with doubts, he shall end in certainties.'[10] Questions are crucial to examining, testing and ultimately strengthening our faith.

FLEXIBLE FAITH

Faith is never static, but active and dynamic. It fluctuates. This is as natural as the ebb and flow of the tide. But what could be more beautiful, more powerful and more lasting than the sea? If the sea were still, it would stagnate. So it is that a faith undisturbed by any waves of doubt becomes spiritually stagnant. Cardinal Basil Hume described faith this way:

> You can go so far paddling in the sea, and there comes a point where it has to carry you. So it is that reason can only go so far, and then comes the point where faith has to carry you.[11]

If we insist on clinging to the misguided notion that, somehow, mature faith in God must represent a state of absolute certainty and stability, beyond the reach of all questioning and doubt, then we have moved it beyond the reach of the vast majority of humanity. Faith in Christ would become a practical impossibility for most people, since few of us ever reach a state that is free from all doubt. *Faith* in Christ has always been, and will forever remain, just that.

Furthermore, an inflexible faith risks not only stagnation but, perhaps most damaging of all, complacency. Unless we are constantly examining what we stand for, what we hold to be precious and significant and what, on the other hand, is mere paraphernalia tacked on to the real truth of the message Jesus taught, then we risk sinking into being too comfortable, too self-absorbed and too self-satisfied to live out an active faith at all.

Jesus told the famous story of the 'Good Samaritan' (Luke 10:25–37), who broke his journey to care for a Jewish man who had been beaten and left for dead on the side of the long road from Jericho to Jerusalem. Jews and Samaritans were normally ethnic and cultural enemies. The first two men to arrive on the scene of the incident were both religious–a priest and a Levite. Neither of the religious men stopped to help the man, a fellow Jew. Why? Ironically, it was because of their strongly held religious views, responsibilities and prejudices. Their question was: 'If I stop to help this man, what will happen to me?' Only the Samaritan–a religious and cultural outsider who would have been looked down upon by the Jerusalem establishment–had the freedom to turn the question on its head and ask himself: 'If I don't stop to help this man, what will happen to him?'

If we are to live out Jesus' teaching as his apprentices, it is vital that, along with questioning our faith, we are also honest enough to question our institutions, our social systems, our judgments, our assumptions and our preconceptions. For unless we have the courage to keep examining the way our faith functions–or malfunctions–we risk presenting to the world only a stale, distorted image of the vibrant reality of Christ's teaching.

GOD MADE IN MAN'S IMAGE

George Bernard Shaw once quipped: 'God created man in his image–unfortunately man has returned the favour.'[12] His comment echoed the work of his contemporary Emile Durkheim, a French sociologist, who suggested that humans worship the gods that they create. Each tribe invents a god who reflects the tribe's values, standards, aspirations, hopes, ambitions and attitudes and then worships that god–thus legitimising and endorsing the tribe's own behaviour.[13]

Many of ancient Israel's surrounding nations, for instance, worshipped pagan fertility gods, which served to affirm and legitimise the selfish desires of the men. For instance, the gods *conveniently* demanded that the men engage in sexual intercourse with religious or 'cultic' prostitutes!

Durkheim's work offers important warnings to us all. The trappings of our twenty-first-century culture too easily entice us–and when they do, our image of God inevitably becomes distorted. We must learn to question our own assumptions and ask: in what ways have we remade God in our own image?

A theology student listened intently to a lecture at his university given by a visiting professor about the search for deeper understanding of the historical Jesus. Eventually, bemused and frustrated, the student couldn't keep quiet any longer. Suddenly, he got to his feet and interrupted the speaker.

'If you scholars have lost Jesus, that's your problem. But I've not lost him. I know him. I don't need to search for him.'[14]

As appealing as this kind of 'shoot from the hip' certainty might seem, it is arrogant and foolish to assume that we have got everything about Jesus 'pinned down' or 'summed up'–that we have no more need to 'search for him.' Questioning is the natural and necessary pursuit for every person–every apprentice – who is not ready to say, 'My understanding is complete.'

BELIEFS CAN BE DANGEROUS THINGS

The perception of absolute certainty is, however, a dangerous thing at more than a personal level. It has often led to violence, terrorism, the dogmatic domination of the vulnerable – and even to war.

The earnest apprentice approached his teacher in search of the truth.

'If what you seek is truth, there is one thing you must have above all else,' began his teacher.

'I know,' said the apprentice. 'I must have an overwhelming passion to acquire it.'

'No,' smiled the teacher, 'what you must have is an unremitting readiness to admit you may be wrong.'[15]

> The power to question is the basis of all human progress.[16]

It was a former archbishop of Canterbury, William Temple, who warned: 'The more distorted a man's idea of God and the more passionately he is committed to it, the more damage he will do.'[17]

Beliefs, when riddled with unexplored assumptions or overzealous conviction, risk becoming dangerous. Questioning is life's alarm bell. At its most ominous, an absence of questioning leads to the formation of manipulative cults–from Jonestown to 'Heaven's Gate'. Those who never question what they believe will tend to believe anything.

The Catholic mystic Anthony de Mello told a haunting story, hinting at the potential dangers of rigid beliefs:

The devil once went for a walk with a friend. They saw a man ahead of them stoop down and pick up something from the ground.

'What did that man find?' asked the friend.

'A piece of truth,' said the devil.

'Doesn't that disturb you?' asked the friend.

'No,' said the devil. 'I shall let him make a belief out of it.'

LEARNING IN COMMUNITY

In Jesus' day, apprentice-learning could not be done by a solitary individual; it required collaboration. Apprentices learned in community with others. An apprentice engaged in dialogue not only with their rabbi but with other apprentices. Through practice, trial and error, discussion, argument, failure, despondency, patience, success and perseverance, an apprentice moved toward greater understanding. Wrestling with questions and doubts was an essential part of spiritual formation.

Ancient Israel functioned as a predominantly oral society. The vast majority of communication was not via written texts, but through face-to-face relationships using the spoken word. Charles F. Melchert, in his book *Wise Teaching*, wrote:

> [Spoken] words cannot be studied like written words ... In a literate world, if I want words, I can find a book and read silently. An oral/aural culture presumes and requires face-to-face presence in a way that a literate world does not ... [spoken] words depend upon the physical presence and cooperation of others ... We who are schooled in literate societies ... tend to forget that the bulk of what we know, especially what we know how to do in living our everyday lives ... [is also] learned and confirmed orally and experientially, rather than from reading. Much of what we do daily continues to make use of orally acquired learning. We seldom look to ... literary productions to provide us with the know-how we need ... So we say, 'My mother always said ...' or 'As Grandpa often said ...' or ... 'My teacher said ...' Such learning is not only cognitively fruitful; it is a rich, holistic, embodied, sensory, and emotional experience that makes for lasting memories.[18]

Oral communication has been the norm throughout history. Indeed, individualised learning is a relatively new idea–it was virtually impossible before the invention of the printing press in the fifteenth century, but still rare even beyond that (the technology was expensive and most people were illiterate).

So every book of the Bible, both the Old and New Testaments, is a communal text for an oral culture. The Old Testament emphasises that teaching, and, therefore, apprenticeships were conducted by word of mouth: '*Tell* your son' (Exodus 13:8). '*Talk* about them when you sit at home' (Deuteronomy 6:7, emphasis added).

Among the early Christian churches, it was groups of believers, rather than individuals, who received the pastoral letters that we now know as the epistles of the New Testament. It was in the context of community that the gospels were read and debated.

None of the New Testament writers ever intended or imagined that people would read their letters alone. When they were read, they were always read aloud in a group setting. Their content was thought about, debated, questioned, discussed, argued over and studied together. Conclusions about their meaning were reached as a collective. Individual insights and perspectives provided balance and alternative points of view.

In this light, it seems probable that each one of us can thrive only within the context where we can ask honest questions and express our real doubts about faith and God, in the security of an open and honest community.

LIVING WITH QUESTIONS

Some beliefs are like walled gardens. They encourage exclusiveness and the feeling of being especially privileged.

Other beliefs are expansive and lead the way into wider and deeper sympathies. As Sophia Lyon Fahs wrote:

> Some beliefs are like blinders, shutting off the power
> to choose one's own direction.

> Other beliefs are like wide gateways opening wide vistas for exploration.
> Some beliefs weaken a person's selfhood. They blight the growth of resourcefulness.
> Other beliefs nurture self-confidence and enrich the feeling of personal worth.
> Some beliefs are rigid, like the body of death, impotent in a changing world.
> Other beliefs are pliable, like the young sapling, ever growing with the upward thrust of life.[19]

Paradoxically, it is only as we constantly struggle with the big questions of believing and faith that we are kept safe from complacency. Am I alone? Does my life mean anything? What should I believe? Can anything help me out of this mess? Have I chosen the right road? When we ask these questions, we aren't getting farther away from faith in God. We're actively renewing our engagement with it. Charles M. Schulz summed up this process:

> Sometimes I lie awake at night, and ask, 'Where have I gone wrong?' Then a voice says to me, 'This is going to take more than one night.'[20]

There are no answers without questions. So, in the end, it is better to live with questions we cannot answer rather than with questions we cannot ask.

The Bible is riddled with questions. Far from being a list of dogmatic statements, it is a rich maelstrom of ideas, ambiguities, explorations, wonderings and doubts; for instance, the books of Job and Ecclesiastes and many of the Psalms. Even Jesus, as he hung on the cross, questioned God, quoting one of the ruthlessly honest Psalms written by King David: 'My God, my God, why have you deserted me?' (Psalm 22:1 CEV). David often demanded answers from God–and admitted that he didn't always get them: 'Why are you so far away? Won't you listen to my groans and come to my rescue? I cry out day and night, but you don't answer, and I can never rest' (Psalm 22:1–2 CEV).

These unflinching cries for help show us that in those moments when we too ask questions of God and wait for an apparently non-existent response, we are not alone.

Far from discouraging or suppressing our doubts, then, the precedents for questioning in the Bible are numerous and are as challenging and uncompromising as any questions you will find anywhere.

But while we can identify with the pain behind all this questioning, perhaps we can also draw hope from the fact that the isolation and frustration were rarely permanent. Ultimately, the very act of voicing the questions often brought some release even if the answers took longer, sometimes much longer, to arrive. As David finally admits in the very same Psalm in which he fired those searing questions at God: 'The LORD doesn't hate or despise the helpless in all of their troubles. When I cried out, he listened and did not turn away' (Psalm 22:24 CEV).

Perhaps it was this sense of hope, drawn from the fact that God listens when we cry out to him, that Jesus was trying to call to mind as he echoed David's words, hanging on the cross.

The Bible does not patronise us with the trite promise that, if we believe, life will hold no mystery or that our doubts will evaporate. Rather, it constantly acknowledges that life is complicated, and that questions are an inescapable and essential part of what it means to be human.

It was a wise man who once said, 'Learn from yesterday, live for today, hope for tomorrow. The important thing is not to stop questioning.'[21]

5

BELONGING

A young man journeys away from his home in pursuit of adventure. One night, while staying in a cheap hostel, he encounters a traveller ravaged by years of sun and drugs. The traveller tells him an improbable tale of a secret island, paradise on earth: the perfect beach, untarnished by tourists.

The next day, the young man finds a piece of paper pinned to his door. It is a hand-drawn map of the island described by the traveller. He sets off to find the island, thinking he has, at last, found the life he has been searching for. Reaching his destination, he finds a small community of other travellers, living in secret. He is welcomed into the group, and the island paradise becomes his new home, its escapism sapping him of all will to return home. Here, he believes, he has found the friendship, freedom and the sense of belonging he has always desired.

Yet beneath the surface, this haven–this heaven on earth–is far less than perfect. The young man slowly realises that what he first believed to be an idyllic society is, in truth, a dangerous, dysfunctional and self-destructive community driven by raw hedonism and self-gratification, with few safeguards on the abuse of power in the pursuit of personal pleasure.

He begins to dream of finding a way back home to the place and the people where he now realises he has always belonged.[1]

We all need to belong. But in our chaotic world, it has become increasingly difficult to feel at home or to find a sense of deep and genuine community with others. Some find it impossible. We live in a culture that often feels acutely impersonal and alienating.

Society has become fragmented. It bears visible wounds of the deep-rooted individualism that has damaged the sense of cohesion and commonality for which communities were once celebrated.

And it is slowly dawning on us that isolation isn't liberation. This pervasive loneliness, a sense of living in exclusion from other people is, along with the drive for significance, one of the most recognisable symptoms of our age. Henri Nouwen described the loneliness:

> Loneliness is one of the most universal sources of human suffering today ... Children, adolescents, adults, and old people are in growing degree exposed to the contagious disease of loneliness.[2]

We are impoverished by this lack of meaningful relationships. As Mother Teresa once remarked, 'Loneliness and the feeling of being unwanted is the most terrible poverty.'[3]

The painful irony is that most of us live in closer proximity to more people than at any other point in history. We are surrounded by people when we work, shop and socialise–but we are lost in the crowd. It would appear that we are losing the ability to build bridges of understanding and communication with one other. As has been wisely observed, in a quote attributed to Albert Schweitzer, 'We are all so much together, but we are all dying of loneliness.'[4]

We have become so preoccupied with ourselves that we simply neglect to build, or don't have time to build, meaningful, mutually supportive relationships. We spend our time pursuing our own agendas, our own fulfilment. Yet, at the same time, the unending quest of every human being is to shatter their loneliness.

No life comes into being in isolation. The mystery of the universe is such that our very formation requires the active participation of others. Even the legacy of our genes is a demonstration of the fact that we are essentially dependent beings. Each one of us is the product of community. Our lives are inseparably bound up with others from the very beginning.

Furthermore, interdependency is a principle which is built into the very nature of the universe. Even a cursory glance at the animal kingdom shows us that interaction is crucial to survival. Not only do members of the same species co-operate–from colonies of ants and bees to herds of elephants and schools of whales–but there is also great interdependency across the diversity of nature's communities. Witness the phenomenon of 'symbiosis'–the bird who gains a free meal by sitting on a hippopotamus and eating the parasites swarming all over it, while the hippo benefits from a good clean. Interdependence is written into the fabric of life.

> The tree needs the soil.
>
> The soil needs the rain.
>
> The rain needs the cloud.
>
> The cloud needs the air.
>
> The air needs the tree.

This interdependency is just as vital to the survival of humanity. As Mike Riddell says, 'It is therefore a bizarre development in the tide of history that we have become so isolated from one another that we have begun to regard our self-contained separation with a certain amount of pride. Those who can function without significant support from others are described as independent and self-reliant, while our desire for relationship is treated as evidence of some weakness.'[5]

Yet it is impossible to be fully human without being with, and committed to, others. We need both to know and to be known. So, held in tension with our drive for individualism and autonomy is, paradoxically, a great longing to belong–to be welcomed, to be valued, not just for what we *do* but for who we *are*.

The delightful contradiction at the heart of all this is the realisation that we can only fully discover who we are as individuals in the context of community. Only as we become aware of the needs of others can we discover what it is to be truly *us*.

A young man lives a thoroughly independent life in the ultimate bachelor pad. Wall-to-wall technology, gadgets and boys' toys are strewn throughout. He is unmarried and unemployed, supported by his inheritance. His greatest concern is maintaining his trouble-free, self-centred lifestyle. He is entirely lacking in hidden depth–and he's proud of it. But he has a persistent question running constantly at the back of his mind–how can someone like him, who thrives on meaningless relationships, ensure that he'll continue to meet beautiful women and yet be absolutely certain they'll dump him before talk of commitment raises its ugly head? A brief encounter with a single mother gives him the perfect answer. He'll chat up single mothers, selling himself to them as their perfect catch. However, after an interlude of sexual bliss, she'll realise that her child isn't ready to have him in their life, leaving him free to ride off into the sunset and go in search of yet another temporary lover.

Things go well until a twelve-year-old boy, the polar opposite of the young man and the son of one of the single mothers he has met, begins to insist on spending too much time with him. Initially he is desperate to get rid of the boy before his credibility and lifestyle are ruined. But gradually the unthinkable starts to happen–he actually begins to enjoy the boy's company. Ultimately, it is this friendship that causes the man to face up to a truth he preferred to ignore: he needs to relate to people at a far deeper level–even if this brings as much pain into his life as pleasure.

The young man's story is this: what he and the dysfunctional lives of the people he meets really need is a real sense of community, because only this can answer their longings.[6]

Our longings and desires can never be fulfilled by isolating ourselves from others. Isolation breeds self-absorption and loneliness. As John Ruskin once said, 'When a man is wrapped up in himself he makes a pretty small package!'[7]

We are designed for relationships, with God and with other people.

LOVE GOD. LOVE OTHERS. THAT'S ALL.

Jesus, like other leading rabbis of his day, taught or interpreted the Torah[8] to his apprentices. Each rabbi's individually crafted interpretation of the Jewish holy book was popularly known as his 'yoke', hence Jesus' famous words in Matthew 11:28–30 to his would-be apprentices:

> Come to me, all you who are weary and burdened, and I will give you rest. Take my yoke upon you and learn from me, for I am gentle and humble in heart, and you will find rest for your souls. For my yoke is easy and my burden is light.

And at the very heart of Jesus' unique yoke were just two liberating principles. For those who had been burdened by the teachings of other rabbis – who often loaded their apprentices with man-made obligations and the crushing weight of religious guilt – Jesus crystallised his interpretation of the Torah into a pair of complementary principles, in Matthew 22:37 – 40:

> 'Love the Lord your God with all your heart and with all your soul and with all your mind.' This is the first and greatest commandment. And the second is like it: 'Love your neighbour as yourself.' All the Law and the Prophets hang on these two commandments.

Interestingly, Jesus' first principle, *Love the Lord your God with all your heart and with all your soul and with all your mind*, is a quote from the fifth book of the Torah (Deuteronomy 6:5), whilst his second principle, *Love your neighbour as you love yourself*, is taken from its third book (Leviticus 19:18). No other teacher before him had ever fused these two great, but isolated, principles together in this way and then gone on to announce that, together, they formed the foundation of the Scriptures while all the rest was, effectively, commentary.

Jesus was teaching his apprentices that if you boiled down the entire Jewish scriptures, distilling them into their basic essence – the message at their core – you were left with this: 'Love God. Love others. Love them the way you love yourself. That's all.'

This is what true religion is really all about. In fact, it's at the heart of what our lives should be about – period.

THE ETERNAL COMMUNITY

The ancient creeds of the church speak to us of the mystery of one God in three persons.

> *We believe in one God,*
> *The Father, the Almighty,*
> *Maker of heaven and earth,*
> *Of all that is,*
> *Seen and unseen ...*
>
> *We believe in one Lord, Jesus Christ,*
> *The only Son of God,*
> *Eternally begotten of the Father,*
> *God from God, Light from Light,*
> *True God from true God,*
> *Begotten, not made,*
> *Of one Being with the Father ...*
>
> *We believe in the Holy Spirit,*
> *The Lord, the giver of life,*
> *Who proceeds from the Father and the Son.*
> *Who with the Father and the Son is worshipped and glorified.*[9]

Perhaps the most profound theological statement in the whole Bible is this: 'God is love' (1 John 4:8). Derek Tidball explains it this way:

> Love is not a quality that God possesses, but the essence of God himself. It is not a minor attribute that characterises God on occasions, but the very heart of God, his essential being. It is not a component part

> of God, but his very nature. Before God is anything else, he is love.[10]

Yet if God had been a single being–if God were 'one' rather than 'three in one'–this profound reality would have been impossible. Stanley Grenz provides this explanation:

> Self-love cannot be true charity; supreme love requires another, equal to the lover, who is the recipient of that love, and because supreme love is received as well as given, it must be a shared love, in which each person loves and is loved by the other. [11]

What the church calls the doctrine of the Trinity tells us that God is a community. Three persons–Father, Son and Spirit, but one in essence–who are defined by their loving relationships with one another.

God exists as a 'tri-unity' of persons in constant internal relationship. God is a society within himself. However, though God is three in one, he always acts as one and lives in absolute unity, without competition or individualism. Colin Gunton, in his book *The Christian Faith*, wrote:

> God is a fellowship of persons whose orientation is entirely to the other ... these three are, while distinct from one another, not in competition, as in modern individualism, but entirely for and from one another.[12]

Since God is a Trinity–a community–this brings new depth to our understanding of what it means for humans to be made in *imago Dei*, 'the image of God' (Genesis 1:27). It means that we only ever realise our full potential as human beings in community with God and with others.

Our capacity for relationships is, therefore, an integral part of what it means to be made in the image of God. But more than this, if God exists as a community, then any individual can never become their true self in isolation. Humanity is designed not simply with the capacity but also with the *need* for community. In a very real sense, we can only find our true selves in relationship with others.

SACRED RELATIONSHIPS

John Donne was, in addition to being a poet, the dean of St. Paul's Cathedral in London. He held a view of a society that was rooted in the life of the Trinity, which he once described as a 'holy and whole college'.[13] It was just before his death in 1631 that he penned the following famous words:

> All mankind is of one author, and is one volume; when one man dies, one chapter is not torn out of the book, but translated into a better language; and every chapter must be so translated ...
>
> As therefore the bell that rings to a sermon, calls not upon the preacher only, but upon the congregation to come: so this bell calls us all: but how much more me, who am brought so near the door by this sickness ...
>
> No man is an island, entire of itself; every man is a piece of the continent, a part of the main ... any man's death diminishes me, because I am involved in mankind; and therefore never send to know for whom the bell tolls; it tolls for thee.[14]

We have a homing beacon within us–the original goodness, or 'god-ness', we were made with. God's fingerprint is still present in each and every life. We may have blurred, distorted and perverted that goodness through our inhumanity, exploitation, violence, greed and self-centredness, but it can never be eradicated.

Human beings are stamped with the image of their Creator, which defines human life as more than merely biological.

However, through our individualism, we learn to affirm ourselves over, against and at the expense of one another and God. As apprentices, learning to walk the way of Christ slowly brings about a process of 'de-individualisation' and, as a result, true 'personalisation'.

This is what Jesus meant when he taught that he had come to bring abundant life–life 'to the full' (John 10:10). Jesus came to help us become fully human–to heal us and make us whole.

God exists as three persons living in perfect relationship and communion; the Trinity is the original and complete community. Because God already lives in a community of perfect love–lacking nothing–it could not have been loneliness that prompted him to create the human race. Rather, it was the perfection of this tri-personal love and interdependence that inspired creation; God created us to *share* in his relationship. C. S. Lewis wrote:

> In God there is no hunger that needs to be filled, only plenteousness that desires to give . . . to be sovereign of the universe is no great matter to God. In Himself, at home in 'the land of the Trinity', he is Sovereign of a far greater realm . . . If I may dare the biological

> image, God is a 'host' who deliberately creates His own parasites; causes us to be that we may exploit and 'take advantage' of Him. Herein is love.[15]

Pope Benedict has commented that the triune God is not a private deity;[16] we cannot create a private fellowship with God. Genuine Christ-centred faith is, of its essence, a trinitarian faith and, therefore, necessitates throwing ourselves into relationship and community with others.

So if we are looking for Christ, we will find him in community with others. Community is the magnifying lens through which our experience of Christ's love is augmented and clarified. And this means that relationships are sacred, for in the context of relationship we can encounter God.

Yet the mystery of the Trinity contains an even more profound truth. God is a community of diversity, not of sameness. God is Father, Son and Spirit. He is not three Fathers, three Sons or three Spirits. While in essence unified, there are distinct differences and unique roles for each person of the Trinity. And so it is that we learn that the deepest community is that which embraces diversity rather than uniformity.

There is something about being in community with those who are different from us that strengthens and completes us. Strong relationships are not based on the removal of differences nor even the mere acknowledgment of those differences, but on embracing and celebrating those differences.

One bird cannot easily protect another from a large predator. But the bulky presence of a hippopotamus does the job just fine. Likewise, no hippo is nimble enough to clean the parasites from another hippo's back. It takes the delicacy of a bird's beak to achieve that. Just as it is in nature, so it is with us: our communities benefit from difference and diversity.

LOVE HURTS

The challenge of human communities is, of course, that people are frustrating–and, ironically, it is often those closest to us who can be the most aggravating. They interfere, make unrealistic demands of us, disappoint us and let us down.

In every relationship, not only are there new opportunities but also new dangers. Every relationship opens us up to the possibility of pain and heartache; to give ourselves to others is always to risk disappointment, rejection and even betrayal. As C. S. Lewis wrote, 'There is no safe investment. To love at all is to be vulnerable.'[17]

It is often our fear of being hurt that holds us back from making ourselves vulnerable and makes the protective shell of isolation look all the more tempting. We are afraid of being dominated or rejected. We are afraid that commitment to others will make us weak. And so, as an act of self-protection, we hold ourselves back.

Willard W. Waller, an American sociologist, said that the greater an individual's love for another, the more vulnerable they become. Those who are more deeply involved in and committed to a relationship end up giving the one that is less involved more power. Waller called this principle 'the principle of least interest.'[18]

This power can be, and sometimes is, used to exploit the other–such as the woman who exploits a man for economic gain or the boy who sexually exploits the girl who is in love with him. The partner with the least commitment to any relationship is always the one who is more likely to exploit the other.

There is, of course, no *safe* way to love. To commit ourselves to others is dangerous. Love never comes with a guarantee of success–it is, of its very essence, a venture of faith.

Many people find themselves caught in a vicious cycle of failing relationships. Phase one is that of infatuation. 'She is wonderful.' 'He is the best friend I've ever had.' The second phase is that of realism. 'I just can't believe that she would say that.' 'If I'd have known that he was going behave like that ...' And phase three is that of rejection. 'I'm never going to speak to her again.' 'I'm having nothing more to do with him.'

Ralph Waldo Emerson summed it up this way: 'Our distrust is very expensive.'[19]

But there is a different way. Between realism and rejection lies another pathway–that of partnership. Though each and every relationship has its points of conflict and agitation, disagreement and difference, these need not be the end of the relationship but rather the beginning of new depths.

BUILDING TRUST

Trust is the basic commodity in any relationship or social interaction. But building trust always involves taking risks.

Trust evolves in any relationship over time. It can't be rushed or hurried. It grows, slowly, over time. Trust doesn't just happen. Instant trust is likely to be the product of a shallow connection or infatuation. True, deep trust–faith in another person–usually takes time, effort, will and work. It is rarely a simple 'on' or 'off' affair. Its ebb and flow are gradual.

Once established, trust can survive great disappointments. But when it is abused, even where it has been developed over years, trust will be damaged. Trust is like money in the bank. The more deposits we make (however small), the more credit we accumulate. However, while one withdrawal will not necessarily take you into the red, if, over time, funds only flow out, eventually even the richest account will be emptied.

Finally, we must recognise that our capacity to love and to trust others depends on our capacity to love ourselves. Jesus taught his apprentices to 'love your neighbour *as yourself*'. A proper sense of love for ourselves is a necessary and vital ingredient when it comes to building healthy relationships. Loving ourselves involves establishing healthy boundaries in our relationships, empowering us to give freely to others without a sense of guilt or obligation. This type of self-love should not be confused with the kind of narcissistic self-centredness that is so destructive to any and every community. For, in the end, it turns out that we can only truly love others when we have learnt to love ourselves as well. When we are truly at peace with ourselves, we can give ourselves to others and discover that we are able to give without losing anything.

And this, again, is why community is essential to human fulfilment and integral to apprenticeship. For it is only in community with others that we can find that elusive acceptance and sense of worth that we so crave. It is this sense of belonging that leads us towards self-acceptance and self-worth.

As the psalmist, in Psalm 133:1 (TNIV), sang:

> How good and pleasant it is when God's people live together in unity!

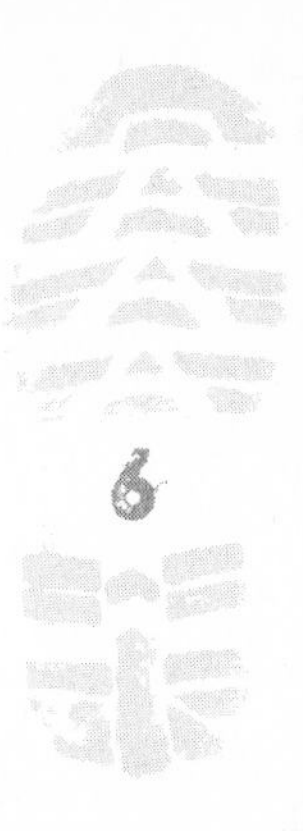

6 SERVING

One day, while wandering through the forest, a teacher stumbled upon a precious stone. He picked it up, dusted it off and put it into his bag.

Some days later he met a traveller and, in conversation with him, opened his bag and showed him the stone. When the traveller saw the jewel, he demanded that the teacher hand it over to him.

The teacher smiled and did so readily.

The traveller departed in a hurry, overjoyed with the unexpected gift of the precious stone that was enough to give him wealth and security for the rest of his life.

However, a few days later he returned in search of the teacher and, finding him, gave him back the stone.

'Now I want you to give me something much more precious than this stone. Give me whatever it was that enabled you to give me the stone in the first place.'[1]

We live in a society where earning and owning are held to be the keys to fulfilment. And, in this kind of emotional climate, the concept that genuine happiness could be derived from serving others will, to some, appear feeble, laughable, even contemptible.

But what if giving, rather than receiving, is the key? What if, in the act of serving–by looking outside of ourselves to the needs of others–we gain more than we could possibly have imagined?

GREED IS THE CREED

There is a children's song in which the lyrics read:

> *Love is something if you give it away,*
> *Give it away, give it away.*
> *Love is something if you give it away;*
> *You end up having more.*
> *It's just like a magic penny;*
> *Hold it tight, and you won't have any;*
> *Lend and spend it, and you'll have so many*
> *They'll roll all over the floor.*[2]

The messages we send to our children tell them that 'tight-fistedness' cannot buy them happiness. The greedy are not liberated by their greed, but imprisoned by it. Those who are selfish misunderstand the purpose of human life.

This message is reinforced by a thousand childhood stories and school assemblies. There's the cautionary tale of the monkey who puts his hand through the railings to steal some nuts only to discover that his hand is stuck when he tries to pull it back. Or the parable about the six-foot-long chopsticks used as utensils in both hell *and* heaven. In hell, each person tries to feed themselves–and starves as a result. But in heaven each person feeds his neighbour; everyone has enough because they choose to serve one another.

In Charles Dickens' perennial classic *A Christmas Carol*, the central character, Ebenezer Scrooge–'a squeezing, wrenching, grasping, scraping, clutching, covetous, old sinner!'[3]–is redeemed only when he is drawn away from his narrow self-interest and obsession with money. The ever-popular stories of Robin Hood, Peter Pan, Hansel and Gretel, Cinderella and the *Chronicles of Narnia* by C. S. Lewis all reinforce the same general point: greed leads to misery, generosity to fulfilment.

But here's the odd thing. Whereas all these childhood stories (and many more) contain a clarity of vision which shows avarice, greed and self-centredness in their true, ugly colours, in the 'grown-up world' we all get used to the belief that real life somehow works differently.

Greed is the creed. Cash is king. The likes of Robin Hood and Bob Cratchit were just naive idealists. And this attitude is confirmed every day in countless commercials, business strategies, movies and conversations.

So we come to learn that our school assemblies were wrong. The truth was to be found in the biology lesson when you were told that life on earth is essentially about the survival of the fittest. It turns out that selfishness–far from being a sin–is actually the universal rule of existence. In the real world, the Scrooges are heroes, the Bob Cratchits are dispensable and the Tiny Tims are unproductive spongers draining the precious resources of the state.

But running counter to this, according to Mike Starkey, are 'those radicals who insist the half-remembered tales of childhood are actually closer to the heart of reality than all the sophistication of the real world. There are those who still cling to the outrageous belief that happiness only comes as we turn real world values on their heads.'[4]

It turns out that many of the world-changing people we most admire have lived by an upside-down minority-report vision of reality: Gandhi, Martin Luther King Jr, Mother Teresa, Nelson Mandela, Desmond Tutu ... to name but a few.

A young girl was suffering from a rare blood disease. Her only hope was to receive a transfusion from someone with exactly the same blood type as hers. After testing various members of the girl's family, it was discovered that her ten-year-old brother had a precise match. The doctor talked to him, gently raising the possibility that he might provide a transfusion for his sister.

'Your sister is dying,' the doctor explained, 'but your blood would save her. Are you willing to give your blood?'

The boy hesitated for a moment. The doctor could see that he was anxious. But then, with a smile, he readily agreed to the process.

After the transfusion, the doctor went to visit the brother to see how he was recovering. As he entered the room, the boy had only one question. 'Tell me,' implored the boy, 'how long will it be until I die?'

Only then did the doctor realise his young patient's misunderstanding, and that he had been willing to give his life so that his sister might live.[5]

THE POWER OF SERVICE

Service–the ability to give freely, without counting the cost–is a concept we admire and, at the same time, find deeply uncomfortable.

There are some who automatically relate 'service' to its unfortunate associations with outdated cultural systems, in which the working classes and ethnic groups are pushed into subservience by the aristocracy or those of a different colour–or both. Forced labour of this kind was, and always will be, a travesty of human rights. Yet the irony is that those inspiring figures who oppose this kind of oppression have, invariably, taken it upon themselves to lay down their own rights in order to serve their fellow humans. Far from perpetuating class systems, learning to serve in this way transcends and even topples them, as has been amply demonstrated to the whole world by Gandhi, Martin Luther King Jr and Nelson Mandela, to name but three.

Indeed, far from being belittled by service, it turns out that we are infinitely enriched by it. This truth is reflected in an early Christian hymn that Paul quotes in his letter to the church in

Philippi: 'In your relationships with one another, have the same attitude of mind Christ Jesus had' (Philippians 2:5 TNIV):

> *Who, being in very nature God,*
> *did not consider equality with God*
> *something to be grasped,*
> *but made himself nothing,*
> *taking the very nature of a servant . . .*
> *he humbled himself*
> *and became obedient to death–*
> *even death on a cross!'*
>
> Philippians 2:6–8

Henri Nouwen reminds us that these words express the core identity of Jesus: 'His self emptying and humiliation are not a step away from his true nature. His becoming as we are and dying on a cross is not a temporary interruption of his divine existence. Rather, in the emptied and humbled Christ we encounter God, we see who God really is.'[6]

The assumption that God is synonymous with power has run throughout history. Many people today, whether they believe in God or not, equate God with power and imagine that power is about the domination of others.

In one of Gary Larson's most famous cartoons, an extremely old, grey-bearded God, sitting in a hi-tech throne room, gazes intently at a closed-circuit television monitor on a desk in front of him. As he watches people go by, his finger is poised over a huge button, around which is writ large one single word–SMITE!

We laugh at Larson's cartoon, but in the popular mind, this is often how the God of the Bible is perceived: a powerful and spiteful punisher of people who stays out of harm's reach, in heaven; 'a bossy, bullying God who wants to keep his laws in order to control us, to lick us into shape, to squash or stifle our humanness or our individuality.'[7]

But when we take for granted this distorted view of divine omnipotence, we miss just how radical a view of God the New Testament proposes. In the famous phrase of the theologian Leonardo Boff, God is 'weak in power but strong in love'.[8]

JESUS THE SERVANT

> It was just before the Passover Feast. Jesus knew that the time had come for him to leave this world and go to the Father. Having loved his own who were in the world, he now showed them the full extent of his love.
>
> The evening meal was being served, and the devil had already prompted Judas Iscariot, son of Simon, to betray Jesus. Jesus knew that the Father had put all things under his power, and that he had come from God and was returning to God; so he got up from the meal, took off his outer clothing, and wrapped a towel around his waist. After that, he poured water into a basin and began to wash his disciples' feet, drying them with the towel that was wrapped around him.
>
> John 13:1–5

As Jesus and his apprentices gathered for the Passover meal (one of the great annual Jewish feasts), it was customary for them to wash the dust from their feet before the meal. Ordinarily a slave would have been present to wash the feet, but because Jesus had asked his disciples to hire a room for the celebration, no such servant was available.

In the ancient world, the washing of guests' feet was the work of slaves. But what is not always appreciated is that foot washing was often regarded as particularly suitable work for women and for female slaves. They were considered the least of the least–the lowest of the low. The extraordinary thing is that even Jewish male slaves were exempt–the only men who were required to wash feet were Gentiles. So foot washing was always performed for a 'superior' by one regarded as an 'inferior'.[9]

There they sat, feet caked in dirt. No one was prepared to break the silence–until Jesus chose to get on with it.

By choosing to wash his own apprentices' feet, Jesus inverted the traditional values of his culture. He humbled himself to do the work of those who were perceived as the lowest on the Jewish social ladder–women, and Gentile and female slaves.

After Jesus had finished washing his disciples' feet, he went on to lay a huge challenge at those same feet–and, by extension, at the feet of all of his apprentices thereafter:

> 'Do you understand what I have done for you?' he asked them. 'You call me "Teacher" and "Lord," and rightly so, for that is what I am. Now that I, your Lord and Teacher, have washed your feet, you also should wash one another's feet. I have set you an example that you should do as I have done for you. I tell you the truth, no servant is greater than his master, nor is a messenger greater than the one who sent him. Now that you know these things, you will be blessed if you do them ...
>
> 'A new command I give you: Love one another. As I have loved you, so you must love one another. By this

all men will know that you are my disciples, if you love one another.'

John 13:12–17, 34–35

Loving one another in this way, in the way that Jesus taught and demonstrated, is tough, because it is about more than words. Washing the feet of others, whether we regard Jesus' words as metaphorical, literal or both, demands a humility and servant-heartedness that is rare, but which is at the very heart of what it means to be an apprentice of Christ.

LOVE IN ACTION

Some years ago, one of the world's greatest ballerinas performed in New York at Carnegie Hall. Her two-hour dance was a profound, moving and magical experience. At the end of the show, the dancer gave a short press conference. In the midst of the barrage of questions, an over-enthusiastic journalist complimented her on the wonderful performance. He went on to ask if, in a short sentence, she could explain the meaning of her dance. The tiny ballerina's response was short and simple: 'If I could have said it, then I wouldn't have needed to dance it!'

All too often, we favour words over action, which inhibits our ability to serve. As Benjamin Franklin once said: 'Serving God is doing good to man, but praying is thought an easier service, and therefore more generally chosen.'[10] We must constantly ensure that our prayer never becomes an excuse for our non-activity and non-engagement.

It was the late 1980s. A young English charity worker flew out to India to see for himself something of the tireless work being carried out by Mother Teresa among the poor and destitute of that country.

Eventually his travels led him to a small hospital she had established in Mumbai. As he wandered around the wards, admiring the work that was being done but emotionally raw from the pain and suffering he was witnessing, he found himself stumbling across the hospital kitchen. Apologising for his mistake, he turned to leave. As he did, one of the cooks took his arm and asked him to sit for a while and rest. 'You have seen enough sorrow for one day,' the cook said. 'Please, stay and have a drink with us.'

Thankful for the opportunity to gather his thoughts and emotions, the young man accepted the kind invitation.

As they talked, it became obvious that the cook had met Mother Teresa personally. 'Tell me,' the young man asked, 'what is she like in person?'

'Small, but full of compassion, selflessness and generosity.'

'But is she more of an ambassador than a hands-on carer?'

The cook laughed. 'Let me tell you a story.'

'Eighteen years ago, a dishevelled alcoholic was brought in to this hospital by Mother Teresa herself. She had found him lying in the gutter. Not an uncommon sight on the streets of India as you will have already noticed yourself. In some ways it's easier to ignore them all than try and help the few you can. What we do here is only a drop in a vast ocean of human need. But then Mother Teresa herself said that the ocean is made up of drops.

'Anyway, for whatever reason, she took special pity on this man. Perhaps she thought he was the most in need, the furthest from human dignity she had seen that day. Or maybe she could see past the degradation, the smell of vomit, the sores and the lice, and see hope, goodness–something redeemable in his life. She asked her driver to stop the car and lifted this almost lifeless soul onto the back seat herself.

'She brought him here to the hospital, where she personally nursed him, day and night. She hardly left his bedside for over a month. She bathed him, fed him, helped him beat his addiction and took care of his every need until he had recovered enough to leave the hospital.'

The young charity worker listened in disbelief at this story. But he also felt a cynical twinge within him. He too had seen homeless people helped, but so many of them had returned eventually to the streets and their addictions–permanent change was difficult to achieve.

'But where is he now?' the young man asked. 'Has he made it?'

The cook smiled. 'I understand your question. But he is okay. I am that man.'

The popular myth is that serving turns you soft. That it robs you of your self-respect, self-worth and dignity; that serving reduces you to a doormat; that it is the product of weakness. However, in reality, the opposite is true. It turns out it is the person who lacks self-esteem who finds it hardest to serve others, to put others' interests first. Self-centred behaviour is a symptom of insecurity–the hallmark of a lack of confidence. Bravado is the blustering of self-doubt. The ability to serve is born not of weakness, but of strength.

Service is a discipline. Far from turning us into pushovers who disregard our self-worth and then invite others to do the same, learning the art and discipline of serving can transform and empower us, helping us to recognise not only *our* worth but also the value of everyone else around us. The more we *give* ourselves–in genuine love of God and of others–the more we *become* our true selves.

WASHING THE WORLD'S FEET

Serving each other, giving our lives for each other, is the liberating principle at the heart of what it means to be an apprentice of Christ. Mother Teresa put it like this:

> We are trying to make bombs of love, of prayer, of sacrifice, to overcome the world by love, and so bring God's love and the proof that God loves the world as a living reality into the hearts of all.[11]

In the late 1700s and early 1800s, a group of friends came together in Clapham, South London, with an extraordinary commitment to serve Christ, one another and those beyond their immediate reach, whom they still recognised as their neighbours. They were all wealthy and influential but had decided to use their resources to achieve their goal. The group, which became known as the Clapham Sect, consisted of business people, politicians, governors, clergymen and a playwright.

The most famous member of the group–William Wilberforce–was a Member of Parliament. On becoming a follower of Christ, at the age of twenty-six, he considered resigning from politics, but John Newton–the former slave trader and author of the famous hymn 'Amazing Grace'–persuaded him to stay and fight for the abolition of slavery.

The Clapham Sect conspired together for the transformation of society. As well as fighting slavery, they worked to ban bull-fighting, improved working conditions in factories, established three major Christian missionary societies, founded an entire country as a safe haven for refugee slaves (Sierra Leone) and started numerous schools.

But every member of the Clapham Sect paid a high personal price to achieve so much. Henry Thornton, a successful banker, is said to have given as much as 80 percent of his income away. On one occasion, Wilberforce was in such danger from the slave lobby that he required an armed guard. He later suffered a nervous breakdown. And it was only days before his death in 1833 that he finally received news of the achievement of his great life goal–the emancipation of slaves across the British Empire.[12]

Czech President Václav Havel argued:

> Genuine politics–politics worthy of the name–the only politics I am willing to devote myself to–is simply a matter of serving those around us: serving the community and serving those who will come after us. Its deepest roots are moral because it is a responsibility expressed through action, to and for the whole.[13]

Oscar Romero of El Salvador was a leader of great courage who ultimately paid with his life for his determination to speak the truth on behalf of his people.

He witnessed the ongoing human rights violations by his country's military government, who harshly repressed any dissent from, or opposition to, their power. By 1980, what had become a civil war–which the UN Truth Commission called 'genocidal'–was claiming the lives of an estimated 3,000 civilians per month. Reports claimed that bodies were clogging streams across the countryside and were thrown in heaps on garbage dumps. Indeed, before the war ended, it claimed the lives of at least 70,000 people.

In a move that instantly won him both the respect of the masses and the enmity of the government, Romero, the country's archbishop, refused to attend any more government functions until the repression of the ordinary people was stopped. The poor, who never expected him to have the courage to take their side, loved him–while the elites of church and state felt betrayed by his stance and afraid of his influence.

'I do not believe in death without resurrection,' he declared a few days before his assassination. 'If they kill me, I will be resurrected in the Salvadoran people.'

The words that sealed his fate, however, were spoken on 23 March 1980, in a nationally broadcast sermon he gave to his gathered congregation. In his message, Romero openly challenged those who, on behalf of the government, were involved in the mass killing of their fellow citizens. As he reached the end of his talk, Romero pleaded with them: 'Brothers, you are from the same people; you kill your fellow peasant ... No soldier is obliged to obey an order that is contrary to the will of God.'

He was inviting the army to mutiny. To thunderous applause, he concluded, 'In the name of God then, in the name of this suffering people I ask you, I beg you, I command you in the name of God: stop the repression.'

The very next day, Romero was gunned down while celebrating Mass. It is said that his blood flowed over the altar.

Just minutes before his life was taken from him, as part of his short homily, Romero was reflecting on the words of Jesus: 'One must not love oneself so much as to avoid getting involved in the risks of life that history demands of us, and those that fend off danger will lose their lives.'[14]

Those who follow Jesus must be willing to serve, regardless of the cost. As Jesus taught his apprentices: 'Whoever wants to save his life will lose it, but whoever loses his life for me will find it' (Matthew 16:25).

The world still needs foot washers.

7

PERSEVERING

On 1 December 1955, Rosa Parks, a black American, was arrested for refusing to give up her seat on the bus she was riding home from work. The now-famous Bus Boycott in Montgomery, Alabama, led by the young Baptist minister Martin Luther King Jr, soon followed. The boycott was to last for 385 days, during which the situation became so tense that King received numerous death threats. On one occasion, he was arrested and his house was bombed.

At the beginning of the boycott, the organising committee set up a voluntary car pool to get people to and from their jobs. King explained that for eleven months this functioned extraordinarily well, but then, in an attempt to break it, the local mayor–Mayor Gayle–instructed the city's legal department to introduce new legislation which would make the operation of the car pool illegal. A District Court hearing to decide the issue was set for Tuesday, 13 November 1956.

The people had willingly suffered for nearly twelve months, but they were tired. King felt that if the car pool was declared illegal, it would be extremely hard to rally the people to walk to and from their jobs. He also knew that if they didn't rise to this challenge, they would be forced to admit defeat.

On the evening before the court case was to be heard, King called the people together. He managed to muster sufficient courage to tell them the truth, then tried to conclude the meeting on a note of hope:

'We have moved all of these months, in the daring faith that God is with us in our struggle. The many experiences of days gone by have vindicated that faith in a marvellous way. Tonight we must believe that a way will be made out of no way.' Yet, in spite of his words, he could feel the cold breeze of pessimism pass over his audience.

In his book *Strength to Love*, King wrote:

> The night was darker than a thousand midnights. The light of hope was about to fade and the lamp of faith to flicker.
>
> A few hours later, before Judge Carter, the city argued that we were operating a 'private enterprise' without a franchise. Our lawyers argued brilliantly that the car pool was a voluntary 'share-a-ride' plan provided without profit as a service by Negro churches. It

> became obvious that Judge Carter would rule in favour of the city.
>
> At noon, during a brief recess, I noticed an unusual commotion in the courtroom. Mayor Gayle was called to the back room. Several reporters moved excitedly in and out of the room. Momentarily a reporter came to the table where, as chief defendant, I sat with the lawyers. 'Here is the decision that you have been waiting for,' he said. 'Read this release.'
>
> In anxiety and hope, I read these words: 'The United States Supreme Court today unanimously ruled bus segregation unconstitutional in Montgomery, Alabama.' My heart throbbed with an inexpressible joy. The darkest hour of our struggle had become the first hour of victory. Someone shouted from the back of the courtroom, 'God Almighty has spoken from Washington.'
>
> The dawn will come. Disappointment, sorrow, and despair are born at midnight, but morning follows. 'Weeping may endure for a night,' says the Psalmist, 'but joy cometh in the morning.' This faith adjourns the assemblies of hopelessness and brings new light into the dark chambers of pessimism.[1]

As King's moving account of this huge first success for the infant civil rights movement attests, finding the strength to persevere in the face of uncertainty, setback and overwhelming opposition, is one of the most powerful resources in our human makeup. Calvin Coolidge, the thirtieth president of the United States, gave this view of what works:

> Nothing in the world can take the place of persistence. Talent will not; nothing is more common than unsuccessful men with talent. Genius will not; unrewarded

genius is almost a proverb. Education will not; the world is full of educated derelicts. Persistence and determination alone are omnipotent.[2]

Perseverance is a determined, resolute hope. Perseverance is an active, decisive attitude of mind, founded on the conviction that steady, peaceful persistence will eventually overcome opposition, intransigence and injustice. And its power is as profound in every circumstance, from the global human rights campaign to the individual apprentice's personal struggle.

King's reference to 'midnight' grew out of his familiarity with, and constant use of, biblical metaphor. One of the parables of Jesus, which King knew well, encourages an attitude of persistence and perseverance. It talks about a man who persists in knocking at his neighbour's door, asking to borrow three loaves of bread. It was this parable that King had in mind while writing about the boycott.

> 'Suppose one of you has a friend, and he goes to him at midnight and says, "Friend, lend me three loaves of bread, because a friend of mine on a journey has come to me, and I have nothing to set before him."
>
> 'Then the one inside answers, "Don't bother me. The door is already locked, and my children are with me in bed. I can't get up and give you anything." I tell you, though he will not get up and give him the bread because he is his friend, yet because of the man's boldness he will get up and give him as much as he needs.
>
> 'So I say to you: Ask and it will be given to you; seek and you will find; knock and the door will be opened

without the tights. Surely dealing with temptation, as, for instance, he did in the forty days he spent fasting in the desert at the beginning of his work as a rabbi, was never going to be any problem for him. Jesus could have gone forty days, forty weeks, forty months or even forty years without food (or, for that matter, water!) in the desert (see Matthew 4).

However, the Bible tells us that Jesus was human in the fullest possible sense. 'He had to be made like his brothers in every way ... Because he himself suffered when he was tempted, he is able to help those who are being tempted' (Hebrews 2:17–18).

Just like us, Jesus encountered the world through the physical realities of a human body and emotions. In Eugene Peterson's wonderful phraseology, '"spirituality" is given skeleton, sinews, definition, shape, and energy by Jesus'.[6]

Jesus aged and experienced hunger, thirst, pain, sorrow, tiredness, joy, pressure, tension, rejection, fear and anger–the full gamut of human feelings, needs and emotions. He lived with all of the functions associated with his physicality–and though it doesn't fit our stained-glass-window idea of him, the consequences of eating and drinking were no less real for him than for us. Jesus was tempted to give up, to turn his back on his mission, in exactly the same way as we are.

Perhaps the most vivid example of this is Jesus' long night in the garden of Gethsemane just before his arrest and crucifixion, where he battled with his desire to walk away from what he knew awaited him:

> Jesus walked on a little way before he knelt down and prayed, 'Father, if you will, please don't make me suffer by having me drink from this cup. But do what you want, and not what I want.' ... Jesus was in great pain and prayed so sincerely that his sweat fell to the ground like drops of blood.
>
> Luke 22:41–42, 44 CEV (see also Matthew 26)

To live intentionally for God, rather than seeking the escape route, was every bit as difficult for Jesus as for those who choose to walk in his footsteps. Jesus was as reliant on the Spirit of God to guide and strengthen him through life as we his apprentices are. Michael Lloyd, in his book *Café Theology*, wrote:

> If Jesus is God living a human life, then we have, in him, the designer's blueprint for how human beings are meant to live. So if we want to know what it would look like to be completely human–human in a way that is unmarred and unscarred by the myriad ways in which we habitually distort our humanity–then it is to Jesus that we must turn.[7]

We are made in *imago Dei*. We are created to be in relationship with God. But that relationship has been weakened, scarred and distorted by our rebellion against God–our deliberate decision to walk *our* way through life instead of his.

In Jesus, we have the ideal model of how life was meant to be lived. Jesus resisted the power of sin. He would not cave in to self-centred living, even under the full power and force of the most intense temptation.

But that raises another question for many of us: a doubt about Jesus and his ability to understand our struggle. If Jesus never sinned, can he truly understand what we are going through?

C. S. Lewis illustrates exactly this point in his book *Mere Christianity*, when he comments that we will often complain that we buckle under temptation simply because we find it so intense that we *cannot* resist. But, says Lewis, in our attitude we make a huge mistake. We wrongly imply that a person who doesn't give in to temptation obviously hasn't felt its power with the same force as we did. 'You just don't know how difficult it is for me,' we protest. But, Lewis reminds us, it is only the reed which stands against the storm and doesn't break that ever feels the full power of the wind – never the one that snaps and lays down flat. The full power of temptation is understood only by those who successfully resist it, not those who give in to its power.[8]

A WORLD AT WAR

Spiritual battles are not just personal and internal. As theologian Walter Wink puts it, 'Our task is to work to change structures as well as individuals.'[9] The church is called to take the sociopolitical nature of evil seriously without minimising its individual and personal aspects. The gospel has implications both for individuals and for society as a whole.

For example, when Jesus taught his disciples to pray: 'Our Father ... your kingdom come, your will be done on earth as it is in heaven' (Matthew 6:9, 10), he was acknowledging that he and his followers inhabited a world where God's will was clearly not done 'as it is in heaven', and that, therefore, they lived day by day with enormous opposition and ongoing struggles. Gregory Boyd, in his book *God at War*, wrote this:

> Jesus' teachings were not first and foremost about high ethical ideals or profound religious insights, though they are frequently that as well. Rather . . . they are about what Jesus himself was most fundamentally about: engaging in mortal combat with the enemy of all that is godly, good and true. In his teachings we find many valuable insights into the nature of the war that ravages the earth, insights that should influence our understanding of the problem of evil.[10]

Both Jesus and the New Testament writers regarded his impending death and resurrection as the means of delivering the decisive victory in this struggle, and are confident of its final outcome. Paul explains that 'having disarmed the powers and authorities, he [Jesus] made a public spectacle of them, triumphing over them by the cross' (Colossians 2:15). But the skirmish goes on. There are battles still to fight.

Paul, in his letter to the Christian apprentices in Ephesus, speaks of their ongoing 'struggle', reminding them that it 'is not against flesh and blood, but against the rulers, against the authorities, against the powers of this dark world and against the spiritual forces of evil in the heavenly realms' (Ephesians 6:12). These authorities and powers manifest themselves through greed, corruption, violence, abuse, war, poverty, hunger and injustice and the systems and institutions which promote and condone them. And, although we know that Christ's cross and resurrection have ultimately defeated these forces, their insidious presence still blights our world.

Part of the mystery of the universe is that God is somehow still engaged in a struggle with the forces of evil, whose greatest desire is to thwart and undermine his will. As C. S. Lewis observed in *Mere Christianity*, 'This universe is at war. But it ... is a civil war, a rebellion, and ... we are living in a part of the universe occupied by the rebel.'[11] Christ calls us to join the battle as we wrestle, pray and work for God's kingdom (kingship) finally to come – in its fullest form – and for his will to be done on earth as it is in heaven.

Harry Boer, who served four years as a chaplain during World War II, spent the final days of that war among Marines in the Pacific theatre. His words offer an instance of the kind of perseverance in the face of evil which Christ's apprentices are called to have: 'The Second Division saw much action, with great losses,' he writes. 'Yet I never met an enlisted man or an officer who doubted for a moment the outcome of the war. Nor did I ever meet a marine who asked why, if victory was so sure, we couldn't have it immediately. It was just a question of slogging through till the enemy gave up.'[12]

Theodore Roosevelt, the twenty-sixth president of the United States, in a speech given in Paris in 1910, said:

> It is not the critic who counts, not the man who points out how the strong man stumbled, or where the doer of deeds could have done better. The credit belongs to the man who is actually in the arena; whose face is marred by the dust and sweat and blood; who strives valiantly; who errs and comes short again and again; who knows the great enthusiasms, the great devotions and spends himself in a worthy cause; who

> at the best, knows in the end the triumph of high achievement, and who, at worst, if he fails, at least fails while daring greatly; so that his place shall never be with those cold and timid souls who know neither victory or defeat.[13]

AFTER MIDNIGHT, MORNING COMES

Apprenticeship to Jesus involves having the courage to struggle forward on our often treacherous journey, rather than retreating into the bland predictability of safety and familiarity. Ultimately, there can be no success without struggle. If we are too afraid to fail, we will never risk enough to succeed.

In 1741 in a small apartment in Brook Street, London, an unemployed and lonely musician sat abandoned. His career had been a rocky one. Once he had been the talk of the town, the man everyone wanted to know. He had dreams and talent. But life hadn't turned out as he'd planned. His hopes had been dashed. He was utterly debt-ridden. He was alone and forgotten; a recluse, lacking motivation, purpose and direction. He didn't know whether he could face the future and even considered suicide as a way out of his misery.

One day a friend called to leave him a script telling the story of Christ–he desperately wanted his friend to take a look at it and comment on it.

But the depressed musician would not even look down into the street from his window to see who was calling up to him. Eventually, frustrated, his friend shoved the whole manuscript, page by page, under the front door and left.

For days the desperate composer couldn't bring himself to look at the manuscript his friend had left, but finally, with nothing else to fill his time, he began to read.

From the start, he was gripped. In the end, he read the whole thing from cover to cover several times – the story of Jesus and the prophecies that predicted his coming. Inspired, he began to compose. For more than three weeks, he didn't stop. He wrote night and day, captivated by the story of Christ – the man who changed the world and transformed so many lives.

So it was that George Frederic Handel composed Messiah and a man, lost and alone, on the edge of surrender, found the new hope that transformed his life.

The honest prayer of Thomas Merton, a Trappist monk and one of the most acclaimed writers on spirituality of the twentieth century, reads this way:

> *My Lord God, I have no idea where I am*
> *going.*
> *I do not see the road ahead of me.*
> *I cannot know for certain where it will end.*
> *Nor do I really know myself,*
> *and the fact that I think I am following your*
> *will*
> *does not mean that I am actually doing so.*
> *But I believe that the desire to please you*
> *does, in fact, please you.*
> *And I hope that I have that desire in all that*
> *I am doing.*

I hope that I will never do anything apart
from that desire.
And I know that if I do this you will lead me
by the right road,
though I may know nothing about it.
Therefore I will trust you always, though I
may seem
to be lost and in the shadow of death.
I will not fear, for you are ever with me,
and you will never leave me to face my
perils alone.[14]

We all live with doubts–of ourselves, of others, of God. There are times for each one of us when it seems as if hope itself has been snuffed out. It is in these moments that we are called to persevere.

'"For I know the plans I have for you," declares the LORD, "plans to prosper you and not to harm you, plans to give you hope and a future"' (Jeremiah 29:11).

Ultimately, the New Testament points beyond our present struggles to God's final, life-renewing victory in which we will share:

> Then I saw a new heaven and a new earth, for the first heaven and the first earth had passed away, and there was no longer any sea. I saw the Holy City, the new Jerusalem, coming down out of heaven from God, prepared as a bride beautifully dressed for her husband. And I heard a loud voice from the throne saying, 'Now the dwelling of God is with men, and he will live with them. They will be his people, and God

> himself will be with them and be their God. He will wipe every tear from their eyes. There will be no more death or mourning or crying or pain, for the old order of things has passed away.'
>
> Revelation 21:1–4

For the apprentice of Christ–who died but who rose again from the dead–we persevere in the certain hope that suffering will be overcome, that death will give way to life. After midnight, morning surely follows.

As Martin Luther King Jr expressed so beautifully: 'Midnight is a confusing hour when it is difficult to be faithful. The most inspiring word that the church must speak is that no midnight long remains. The weary traveller by midnight who asks for bread is really seeking the dawn. Our eternal message of hope is that dawn will come.'[15]

8

FORGIVING

A young man named John had left his family home after one too many arguments with his father. Disagreements between them were common. They were both passionate and fiery. Eventually, their arguments went too far. Before they knew what had happened John had wished his father dead, to which his father retaliated that, as far as he was concerned, their relationship was already dead. Shortly afterwards, John stormed out of the family home with a small bag of possessions and a handful of savings. That was the last they saw or heard of one another for more than a decade.

It took a long time, but eventually the father's stubbornness waned. Being right wasn't nearly as important as being reconciled to his son.

It was the day of the twelfth anniversary of that fateful argument, and John's father could bear the separation no longer. Now an old man, he decided to make the journey to the city where he believed his son was living. For several days, he wandered around the streets talking to people, showing them pictures of his son in the hope that someone would recognise him.

One evening, John's father sat in the lobby of the hotel where he was staying and read the local newspaper. As he read, an idea formed in his mind. The next day he took out an advert in the same newspaper which simply read, 'John. All is forgiven. Please meet me in Central Square, outside the railway station, next Wednesday, 7.00 pm, Dad.'

A few days later the advert was published, and the following Wednesday evening, John's father made his way towards the square as promised. His emotions were mixed. Would John have seen the advert? Was he really living here? What if he couldn't find it in his heart to forgive his father for the things he had said? Was this all just a waste of time? Could he really hope for a reconciliation?

As the old man neared the square, there seemed to be more hustle and bustle than normal. Perhaps there was an event which he had failed to take into account. Maybe he would miss his son because of the crowds. The square was packed. 'This is an impossible task,' he thought. 'How will I find him in such a sea of faces?'

However, having come this far, the anxious father was desperate not to miss possibly his only chance of being reconciled with his son. So, climbing aloft a statue in the middle of the square, he shouted at the top of his voice, 'John!'

And a sea of tear-stained faces turned towards him.

The act of forgiving is one of the toughest challenges any human being ever faces. Yet it's also one of the most liberating acts we can perform. Far from leaving us weak, forgiveness is empowering both to the giver and the receiver. When we choose not to forgive, we become chained to the anger of the past. But forgiveness brings freedom–freedom not only for the recipient of our forgiveness but also for ourselves.

Some years ago, I met a couple whose only daughter had been killed in a hit-and-run accident whilst out riding her bike. When eventually arrested, the driver responsible was discovered to have no license–it had been revoked as a result of a prior dangerous driving conviction–and no insurance.

After the trial, the driver was sent to prison for manslaughter. But for the girl's parents, prison was not enough.

After his daughter's killer had served his sentence and was released, the girl's father borrowed a gun and shot him as he stepped through the prison gates.

Amazingly, the man survived. The dead girl's father, however, was arrested for attempted murder. At his trial he confessed that he had, indeed, wanted to kill his victim, and that the only remorse he felt was that he had not succeeded in his attempt to gain revenge for the death of his daughter. However, in spite of this confession, the father was acquitted. The jury found the driver–who had never once shown the slightest sign of remorse for the life he had taken–so repulsive that they delivered a unanimous verdict of 'not guilty'.

But the story doesn't end there. Even this was not enough for the girl's parents. For them, things were still far from resolved. Rather than finding release from their bitterness through the retaliation they had already exacted, they became even more consumed with the thought of revenge.

Some time later, I had the opportunity to ask the girl's mother if she wished her husband had succeeded in his attempted murder. Her chilling reply still haunts me. 'No,' she snarled. 'I need to pull that trigger myself. I need to watch him die and know that *I'm* responsible.'

The ancient approach of retaliation is as popular as ever.

EYE FOR EYE, TOOTH FOR TOOTH

'Retaliation' comes from the Latin word *talis*, meaning 'like' or 'such'. By its very definition, retaliation is the practice of matching like for like. Its doctrine is simple: 'Let the punishment fit the crime,' or, as Deuteronomy 19:21 defines it: 'Life for life, eye for eye, tooth for tooth, hand for hand, foot for foot.'

However, as Old Testament ethicist Chris Wright explains: 'Possibly no other Old Testament text has been the victim of more misunderstanding and exaggeration than this one.'[1]

The 'eye for an eye' principle is ever popular and still used, even today, as a justification for retaliation as an approach to conflict resolution. However, within its original cultural setting, the teaching on retaliation played a very different role. What is often misunderstood is that, rather than encouraging retaliation, Deuteronomy 19 provides a unique ethic of constraint which was put in place to curb, rather than to justify, excessive violence and vengeful punishment. It was designed and intended to limit, rather than encourage, revenge. So, instead of giving us a *mandatory* sentence, the law existed to set a *maximum* penalty beyond which it was unjust to go.

The nations of the ancient Near East worshipped numerous gods whose vengeful characters and behaviour 'legitimised' similar violent actions from their followers. As a nation, Israel grew up surrounded by these cultures and their seductive influence. Thus, the Old Testament is the unfolding account of Yahweh's plan to reveal his true character and, through this, to change the beliefs, values and behaviours that dominated the ancient world.

Imagine that the people of Israel had a bucket with the name 'god' inscribed on it. Into this bucket they poured all their ideas about the character of the divine. The story of Israel is really the story of how Yahweh – the true God of the whole earth – works away at getting the people of Israel to empty out the distorted, cruel, vengeful and pagan ideas with which they had filled their 'god' bucket and replace them with contents that more truly reflect his generous and forgiving nature. It was the reality of this nature that, ultimately, was fully expressed through Jesus, who told his followers that he had come not to destroy the Old Testament law but to fulfil, or explain, its central truth. Jesus came to bring *clarification* to the law, not a *contradiction* of its teaching. (See Matthew 5:17.)

In the words of N. T. Wright, the New Testament 'continually presents the Old Testament as *an unfinished story*, and shows that it invites and even requires a final chapter ... Jesus himself.'[2]

THE POWER OF NOT HITTING BACK

In what we now know as Jesus' Sermon on the Mount, Jesus declared: 'You have heard that it was said, "Eye for eye, and tooth for tooth." But I tell you, Do not resist an evil person. If someone strikes you on the right cheek, turn ... the other also' (Matthew 5:38–39).

If we are honest, this announcement seems absolutely ridiculous. Why on earth should we let someone openly abuse us without fighting back?

However, Jesus' words would have had a completely different impact on his original audience, who could not have failed to appreciate just how empowering this new teaching was. Everybody who heard Jesus' words would have known exactly what he was talking about.

The people Jesus addressed were, for the most part, used to being pushed around and put down. They were some of the lowliest people in Israel's segregated society, all too used to enduring regular verbal and physical abuse from their 'superiors'. One method commonly employed by ruthless masters was to humiliate their 'inferiors' with a quick flicked backhand slap across the face. The slap was designed not so much to injure as to insult, belittle and degrade them. A master would backhand his slaves; a husband would slap his wife; a Roman a Jew; and so on.

In Jesus' society, it was culturally unacceptable, indeed unthinkable, to use your left hand for anything but 'unclean' tasks related to using the toilet. This taboo meant that people would intuitively use their right hand for most tasks without even thinking about it. Indeed, there are a number of cultures today in which this is still the case. In Western culture, we still naturally (and traditionally) use our right hand, not our left (whether we are right- or left-handed), to greet people.

A controlling and aggressive 'superior' would therefore backhand slap a servant with his *right* hand – striking them across their *right* cheek. So, when Jesus taught his oppressed hearers to turn the other cheek (so that their *left* cheek faced their aggressor), he was suggesting that instead of taking the insult they had suffered lying down, they should assert themselves. To that end, notice that he does not suggest that they present their aggressor with the same cheek (the right cheek) again.

By following Jesus' advice and presenting their left cheek, a servant would make it impossible for the master to hit them again with the back of the right hand. Even though the servant's left cheek would now offer a perfect target for another blow, it meant the aggressor only had one option. Unable to use his 'unclean' left hand, he would have to use his right forehand or fist to strike his victim. Doing this presented a cultural problem. Only equals fought in this way. If the master wanted to continue to hit the servant, he could do so only by acknowledging his servant as an equal.

And that was precisely Jesus' point.

Far from representing a 'lay-down-and-die' passivity, turning the other cheek is a subversive action born of inner strength. Through it, the 'victim' of the aggression was effectively saying, 'I'm a human being, just like you. I refuse to be humiliated any longer. I am your equal. And if you want to hit me again, you are going to have to acknowledge that.' So, rather than teaching 'just take it', Jesus urges assertive, non-violent resistance: 'Stand up for yourself, take control.' But, critically, at the same time, he is teaching his would-be apprentices to break the cycle of aggression from a position of strength: 'Don't give in–but don't hit back.'

The way of Jesus is, therefore, neither cowardly submission nor angry reprisal. It is about bold, energetic and even costly action. Forgiveness is not for the cowardly or weak-kneed. It is the response of the strong–those with a sense of self-worth and courage.

One of the big traps we fall into is to think of Jesus' illustration, and those that follow it–giving your cloak away and going the extra mile (see Matthew 5:40–42)[3]–as an exhaustive list. Having done this, many reject it as idealistic and irrelevant to us and our culture.

It is vital to understand that these were just sketches. Jesus offered a few examples of simply hundreds of imaginative and effective ways that people could take on injustice without allowing resentment to boil up inside them, without destroying their dignity, without resorting to reprisal and revenge. And, of course, Jesus' audience knew that such tactics could seldom be repeated. In fact, the power of a non-violent response is often in the element of surprise. These tactics work because of their shock value.

The idea is to stay one step ahead of those who oppress or upset us, to be creative in finding new ideas for rejecting passivity and resisting evil without allowing bitterness to control our responses.

Reflecting on Jesus' teaching, Martin Luther King Jr, who found numerous ways during his lifetime to turn the other cheek,[4] summed things up famously in this way: 'An eye for an eye leaves everyone blind.'[5]

REVENGE IS NEVER SWEET

Retaliation and revenge, even if exacted 'moderately', never allow wounds to heal. Revenge helps nobody. However tough it may be, it is only through forgiveness that real healing can begin to occur and real peace be found.

Forgiveness is the only winning solution. Choosing to rise above the cycle of 'tit-for-tat' behaviour is the only route to well-being. Hatred engenders more hatred in a downward spiral of mutual resentment and reproach. It is a descending spiral, begetting the very thing it seeks to destroy.

> Whoever opts for revenge should dig two graves.
>
> CHINESE PROVERB

Jesus said, 'All who draw the sword will die by the sword' (Matthew 26:52). Or, as Carl Jung, the noted Swiss psychiatrist, poignantly observed, 'You always become the thing you fight.' The pull of hatred is strong, a powerful force that can often change us in harmful ways. In Romans 12:17–20, Paul advised:

> Do not repay anyone evil for evil ... If it is possible, as far as it depends on you, live at peace with everyone. Do not take revenge, my friends ... On the contrary: 'If your enemy is hungry, feed him; if he is thirsty, give him something to drink.'[6]

Revenge can never resolve anything; rather, it is a vicious, self-perpetuating cycle, leaving in its wake a trail of destruction. So, like a contagious disease, it has come to blight our world. As Martin Luther King Jr reminds us in *Strength to Love*: 'Returning hate for hate multiplies hate, adding deeper darkness to a night already devoid of stars.'[7]

FORGIVENESS HEALS

Bitterness eats away at us; it is a sickness and, indeed, can manifest itself as such. Holding on to anger and resentment has a disastrous impact on our well-being. It's like a ticking time bomb waiting to explode inside us. There is substantial evidence to suggest that bearing a grudge aggravates illness and undermines health. Many of us know all too well that stress can cause an ulcer or a migraine, but we often fail to see the relationship between our capacity for forgiveness and our mental, physical and spiritual wholeness in a wider sense. Forgiving heals us not only emotionally but physically too.

Clinical research undertaken by psychologists Robert D. Enright and Everett L. Worthington Jr demonstrates that for the person who offers forgiveness, there is not only a noticeable reduction in 'anger, depression, anxiety, and fear' but also a number of 'cardiovascular and immune system benefits.'[8] Put bluntly, people who bottle up their resentment are far more susceptible to suffering than those who are able to defuse it by translating their emotions into acts of forgiveness. An Amish farmer described it with these words:

> The acid of hate destroys the container.[9]

Enright and Worthington identify two types of forgiveness: decisional and emotional. They define decisional forgiveness as a deliberate, conscious commitment to control negative behaviour even if negative emotions continue. Though decisional forgiveness promises not to act in revenge, it doesn't necessarily make the person who chooses this action feel any less angry.

In Matthew 6:12, Jesus teaches his apprentices to pray: 'Forgive us our debts, as we forgive our debtors' (KJV). This refers to a determined act of decisional forgiveness, just as turning the other cheek would have done.

The act of loving my enemy does not mean feeling 'all gooey' about them. Though a decision to forgive does not mean that bitter feelings are automatically or instantly erased, it does mean that emotional transformation is more likely to follow.

Emotional forgiveness happens when negative emotions—resentment, hostility and even hatred—are slowly replaced by positive feelings. The chains of bitterness are broken. This often takes time; the emotional effects are rarely immediate.

Thus, forgiveness is both a short-term act and a long-term process.

A young woman was raped and beaten, and her boyfriend was shot in the head. In the aftermath of the initial shock, the last thing on her mind was forgiving her attackers. But when one of them was sentenced to death, she knew she couldn't go on feeling bitter. For this girl, the issue was never about her attackers. It was about her. 'It took a long time for me to accept the fact that my life would never be the same–and it was in that process that I encountered the need to forgive ... That's the only thing that takes away the anger and pain and restores the peace ... People ask, 'Why do you even have a need to forgive your attacker? He doesn't deserve your forgiveness.' But what he deserves is not the problem I'm trying to solve ... When I forgive, I'm the one who benefits.'[10]

> You have heard that it was said, 'Love your neighbour and hate your enemy.' But I tell you, love your enemies and pray for those who persecute you, that you may be children of your Father in heaven.
>
> MATTHEW 5:43–45 TNIV

Jesus' words, 'Love your enemies', probably amount to the most admired and least-practised piece of teaching in history. More often than not, they are viewed as impractical idealism. Extraordinarily, no such charge is ever made against violence and bitterness in spite of the fact that history has proved, time and again, that revenge solves nothing.

CHOOSING TO FORGIVE

The principle of forgiveness, as taught by Jesus, has been embraced by hundreds of persecuted minorities throughout history: from the earliest Christians to followers of Tolstoy,

Gandhi, Martin Luther King Jr, and the black churches of South Africa. These groups have all demonstrated that forgiveness, however difficult, is the only way to break ongoing cycles of vengeance. King, in his book *Strength to Love*, wrote:

> We must develop and maintain the capacity to forgive. Whoever is devoid of the power to forgive is devoid of the power to love ... Forgiveness does not mean ignoring what has been done or putting a false label on an evil act. It means, rather, that the evil act no longer remains as a barrier to the relationship. Forgiveness is a catalyst creating the atmosphere necessary for a fresh start and a new beginning.[11]

Developing this capacity to forgive means, first of all, accepting that life is unfair. A commonly held assumption is that forgiveness should be about fairness. Many believe that we can contemplate forgiveness only *after* justice is done, once we have 'got even'. But it is this type of 'fairness' that preaches 'an eye for an eye'. Forgiveness is, in fact, the act of pardoning the deliberate wrong that has been done *without* seeking punishment, compensation or even apology. Where possible, it even involves embracing and being reconciled to the person responsible. Forgiveness of this kind is not 'fair'. It is an enormous challenge. But it is immeasurably worthwhile.

Though forgiving can be seen as an occasional noble act, its true benefits are discovered as it becomes a continuous attitude of life. Forgiveness is the wisest approach, not just to life's major hurts but to the ongoing minor repetitious irritations of everyday life as well. Indeed, it is our response to these everyday events that slowly but surely shapes our character.

The myth that community is soft and cuddly, snug and cosy, is, at best, a romantic fiction. At worst, it is an outright lie. Make no mistake. Being part of a community – any community or family – is painful, which is a major reason why so many people just won't commit to others.

A teacher asked his apprentices how best to judge whether the darkness of the night had ended and day had dawned.

'When you see the first eagle take to the sky,' volunteered one apprentice.

The teacher shook his head.

'When you see the mist lift from the field,' suggested another.

The teacher lowered his eyes.

'Tell us then,' asked the apprentices, 'is there any sign that we can trust?'

'When you can look into the eyes of any man or woman and recognise them as your brother or sister, only then has dawn come,' replied the teacher.

'If you cannot do this, then however bright the sun is shining, it is still night.'

Community is a source of tension as well as tenderness, resentment as well as respect, aggravation as well as appreciation, pressure as well as pleasure and friction as well as friendship. Every community makes us vulnerable to pain and sometimes leaves us feeling battered and bruised, brutalised and even betrayed.

In this context, C. S. Lewis points out how we often confuse forgiveness with excusing. He wrote that people often talk about forgiving someone by *excusing* what they did, on the basis that they couldn't help, or didn't mean, what they said or did. But Lewis points out the flaw here: 'If one was not really to blame then there is nothing to forgive.'[12] Therefore, the pinnacle of forgiveness is reached when we forgive someone *even though* there is absolutely no excuse for their words, attitude or behaviour. Genuine forgiveness begins when there are no excuses left. Lewis wrote:

> Real forgiveness means looking steadily at the sin, the sin that is left over without any excuse, after all allowances have been made, and seeing it in all its horror, dirt, meanness and malice, and nevertheless being wholly reconciled to the person who has done it. That, and only that, is forgiveness.[13]

It is precisely this type of forgiveness that we are offered by God. He celebrates our strengths and sees our weaknesses–all our 'horror, dirt, meanness and malice'. Yet he loves us and forgives us.

Knowing that God both loves and forgives us frees us to learn how to forgive others. Offering forgiveness is never easy. Yet we who have been forgiven so much are called to offer mercy to those who have offended us. As Paul phrased it in his letter to the community at Colossae: 'Bear with each other and forgive whatever grievances you may have against one another.

Forgive as the Lord forgave you' (Colossians 3:13). Or, as Alexander Pope wrote:

> To err is human, to forgive, divine.[14]

Forgiveness does not condone the wrong. It does not deny the pain inflicted. It gains power over the evil we have experienced by choosing to leave it behind. Though we may remain deeply wounded, we choose to forgive through a conscious act of will.

To resent is to lose. To retaliate is to lose control. But to forgive is to win. Gerard Kelly, in his poem 'I Choose to Forgive' from *Spoken Worship*, writes this:

> *Though the walls of my heart are broken*
> *and the centre of my self is black-bruised*
> *by the lash of the lies that you've spoken*
> *and the wounds of the words that you've*
> *used,*
> *though I huddle, a tear-trembling tragedy*
> *stripped of the power to trust,*
> *blocked off from all who might help me*
> *by the guilt that came wrapped with your*
> *lust,*
> *I choose to forgive.*
>
> *And this act alone*
> *breaks the cycle.*
> *This act alone*
> *rights the wrong.*
> *This act alone*
> *ends the evil.*

This act alone
makes me strong,

heals blind hatred with soft sight,
kicks the darkness into light.[15]

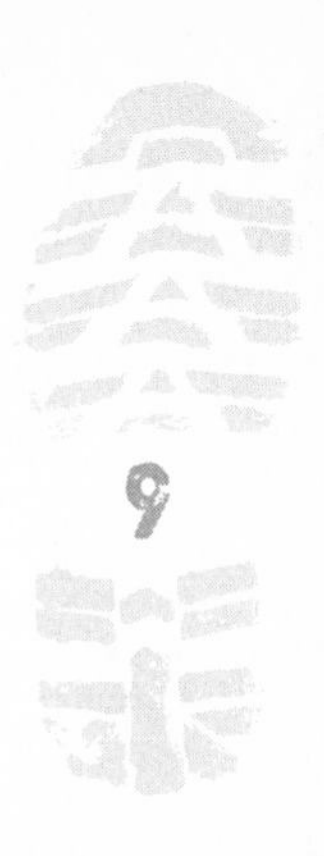

LISTENING

An apprentice asked his teacher, 'How can I find peace in such a noisy town? Every time I try to meditate, I am distracted by the noise.'

The teacher took the apprentice to a lake. 'What do you see when you look at the lake?' he asked.

The apprentice looked at the surface of the water. The wind was whipping it up into choppy waves.

'It is troubled,' he said.

'Then dive to the bottom,' said the teacher.

Hesitating for a moment, the apprentice duly took his teacher's advice and dived into the turbulent waters.

After a time he surfaced.

His teacher asked him again, 'What do you see when you look at the lake?'

'It is deep and still,' he replied.

'So then, you must learn from the lake!'

Life is frantic and chaotic. Our time is squeezed.

Why is it that we tend to shy away from the very thing that we need most? Our lives are filled with noise and distraction. But when left alone with our thoughts, we do everything we can to escape the very peace and solitude we claim to crave. Erwin McManus, in his book *Soul Cravings*, described it this way: 'Sometimes the thing we want the most, we fear the most.'[1]

What are we afraid of? Perhaps we are scared of facing up to the honest truths with which stillness confronts us. Or it may be that, for some of us, the attractions of the surface are more appealing than the silence of the depths.

They say that the universe 'whispers'. Some scientists conjecture that this is the residue of the Big Bang. But even though this whisper has been there for an eternity, it has only recently been heard. Astronomers have patiently listened, blocking out every other sound around them, and tuned their radio telescopes to listen to the hiss, to the whisper of the universe.

But there is another 'whisper' that has permeated the fabric of the universe for an eternity: the voice of God.

If we have ears to hear, we can sense God whispering to us in a multitude of ways: through the beauty of the sun as it rises over the warm seas, the ice-cold glory of the mountain range, the moon-lit night sky, in the smile of a friend, the cry of a newborn baby, the memory of a treasured experience.

But we can also hear God in the dark and disturbing experiences of life. As Martin Luther, the father of the sixteenth-century Reformation movement within the Christian church, came to understand, God is 'the God of the humble, the miserable, the afflicted, the oppressed, the desperate, and of those who have been brought down to nothing at all.'[2]

But those who do not listen will hear ... nothing.

STILL

A man lived a life of humble poverty.

However, every day he faithfully prayed the same prayer: 'Lord, take pity on me and grant me a life of wealth and comfort.'

He prayed this same prayer every single day for some years, remaining ever confident that God would eventually grant his request.

However, after many years, his priorities began to change.

Slowly he became far less interested in wealth or comfort and much more concerned with learning to serve others and meet their needs. Indeed, he devoted his life to prayer and service and even took to the habit of giving the majority of his small income away.

One day, as he prayed, he heard the voice of God.

'I have decided to grant your prayer,' God told him.

The man looked shocked. He thanked God for his generosity but explained that his interests had now changed, and he no longer wished for either wealth or comfort. 'But, there is one thing I would really like to know,' the man ventured. 'Why has it taken you so long to hear my prayer?'

'I knew your prayer even before you prayed it,' God replied. 'But out of my love for you I have refrained from granting it.'

And the man understood exactly why God had done so.

Many people think prayer is essentially about asking, about trying to get what we want from God, about making demands of him, about pleading with him to let us have our own way. Our prayers become little more than shopping lists. 'Give me what I want, now.'

In Jesus' famous story of the lost son, we learn about a young man who, bored with his lot, decides to leave home. Consumed with his own desires, he demands of his father: 'Give me what is mine ... now!' Then he walks away, with his pockets full, to live *his* life *his* way. It is only after he has squandered his wealth and been abandoned by his new-found 'friends' that his attitude changes. In his brokenness, he comes to his senses and decides to turn homeward. On his return, his heartfelt request to his father is simply this: 'Make me your servant.'

Now that's a prayer!

God will not force himself on us. He gives us the space we demand, and then, like the father in the parable, he waits patiently, day after day, month after month for our return. Erwin McManus, in his book *Soul Cravings*, describes it like this:

> We run from God because we long to be loved and we have convinced ourselves that the One who is most loving could not and would not embrace us.[3]

God, we discover, not only allows but encourages our freedom. He grants each one of us the space to explore our own pathway through life. Yet he waits, watches and hopes for our return. And once we begin the journey towards him, just like the father in Jesus' parable, he rushes out to greet us and throws a party. The God of the Bible is not a God of reprisals and 'I told you so's'. He is the God of love, who loves us as we are and who welcomes us home with joyful celebration.

Indeed, understanding that God loves us is the first step on the journey home. But there are many distractions along the way. How often do we become still enough to edit out the 'white noise' of everyday life that so easily drowns out the whisper of God? Much of our lives are spent rushing from one hectic day to the next without much thought of stopping to listen or to reflect on the trajectory of our journey. In Psalm 37:7 we are told:

Be still before the LORD and wait patiently for him.

Rushing headlong through life, without pause for reflection, is a sure way to get lost. Taking the time to find the right path can make all the difference between a successful journey and a disaster. If you've ever been lost in the dark, you'll know that it's a good idea to sit still long enough to listen, strain your eyes, and watch for any clues which might help you locate your position.

The distance between praying 'give me' and 'make me' is often the long and painful journey home.

FINDING THE DESERT

Prayer is the discipline of creating space in which God's voice can be heard.

It is a *carpe diem* world. We are told to 'seize the day', to make the most of our lives. But seizing the day is more than just cramming as much into life as we can. True and lasting fulfilment doesn't come from rushing through life, one experience after another, barely stopping to take a breath. The secret to a fulfilling journey is having the wisdom to pause long enough to savour the experience.

A farmer paused from his work in his apple orchard.

He made his way towards the farmyard and his favourite bench in the sun. He smiled, sat back and lit his pipe.

A few minutes later, a young executive salesman pulled up in a smart car and got out.

'Good morning. Are you the owner?' he enquired rather impatiently.

'Well, yes ... I guess I am. How can I help you?' the farmer responded.

'The question is, rather, how can I help you!' came the confident reply from the man in the suit. 'May I ask you what are you doing?'

'I'm having a rest,' replied the farmer.

'Don't you think you should be busy?' said the salesman, glancing down at his watch.

'Why?' asked the farmer.

'That's exactly why I'm here to see you,' enthused the salesman. 'My company can help you by putting together a business plan and then enabling you to borrow the money to invest in new equipment and systems which will bring you greater efficiency and improved productivity.'

'Why should I want to do that?' asked the farmer.

'Because, by developing your business, you will be able to reach a place where you can afford others to work for you and build your team.'

'What would I do then?' enquired the puzzled farmer.

'Well ... then you could take it easy, relax and enjoy life.'

The farmer smiled. 'That's what I'm doing now.'

The ancient art of forming healthy routines or patterns of life developed over the centuries within the movement known as 'monasticism'. Christian monasticism first appeared in the eastern part of the Roman Empire. The Desert Fathers, as the first monks were called, were hermits and ascetics who inhabited the desert of Egypt in order to flee the chaos and persecution of the Roman Empire.

Even when Christianity was given legal status throughout the Roman Empire by Constantine and his co-emperor in the East, Licinius,[4] some Christians continued to live in these marginal areas. The solitude of the desert life remained attractive as a means of learning self-discipline. Many monks saw a model for their ascetic approach to life in the fasting of Jesus in the desert. They believed that desert life would allow them to hear God's voice and follow his pathway through life in a more intentional way.

Around 500 AD, a young Italian by the name of Benedict of Nursia was inspired by the stories of these early hermits. Benedict decided to give up the comfort of his student life in Rome and become an ascetic monk, living as a hermit in a cave. In time, he began to attract a number of disciples. This was not what Benedict had initially intended for himself and, inevitably, relational struggles and tensions developed within the community of disciples that formed around him. Learning from this experience, Benedict made the decision to found a monastery, progressing from the unstructured nature of desert life to an organised, involved community. It was in this context that Benedict wrote his now famous *Rule of Life*[5] to bring a sense of clarity and stability to community life. He understood that isolation had its limits and that building a deep relationship with God entails listening to him, not by detaching ourselves from others but through forging relationships with them.

A RULE OF LIFE

When many people hear of Benedict's *Rule*, they immediately imagine a book of harsh regulations and strict laws that govern monastic life. But his work is nothing of the sort. In fact, what he produced was a book of helpful, down-to-earth insights about living as Christ's apprentice in the context of a community. The *Rule* is a series of practical suggestions or measures (hence the term *rule*, as in measurement) on how to create a set of priorities–a rhythm of life–which allows the time to listen to God and to demonstrate loving commitment to others.

What we commonly call spiritual 'disciplines' or 'rules' are simply ways in which apprentices of Christ can learn to walk in his way of life. These disciplines are the types of activities in which Jesus engaged to nurture his own relationship with God–times of solitude and silence away from the crowds, the study of Scripture, times of prayer, generosity in giving time and energy to serve and engage with others.

Since the time of Benedict, other apprentices of Christ have developed a rich diversity of personal rules or rhythms and patterns of life, each with its own distinctive emphasis. These practices are frequently shaped by their unique character and personality, but they have the same goal as those of Benedict: nurturing a lifestyle which includes enough space in which to be alert to the whisper of God.

Basil Hume was the cardinal archbishop of Westminster from 1976 until his death in 1999. At the age of eighteen, he became a Benedictine monk (a follower of Benedict's pattern for life). Learning from Benedict, he wrote:

> Meditation is what we do when we steal moments out of the day to be alone with God, however short that time may be; when we wonder what he is like, when we 'explore' God. But we need something to guide us in our exploration. There can be no better starting point than a passage from the Gospel, reading it slowly until it gives up its meaning; then it stirs your heart. When you start to meditate, you will find distractions galore, even boredom, the sense of getting nowhere. The point is you have to stick at it. You have to make an act of faith, because the moments you spend trying to raise your mind to God are precious and golden.[6]

LEARNING TO LISTEN

Some years ago, I was speaking at an event after which a crowd of people gathered around me to ask questions. As a result, I only half remember the young girl and her mother who pressed a piece of paper into my hand before hurrying off. It was not until the end of the day, when I finally got a chance to sit down on my own, that I looked at that piece of paper. It was a simple drawing of a palm tree in the sun with a text, in bold-coloured pen, that read: '"Be still and know that I am God" To Steve from Emily.'

I still have that simple picture–in fact I sat in my study and looked at it again this morning. In the busyness of my journey through life, it has become a valuable symbol and signpost for me. Not only does it remind me to slow down, it has become a vehicle that enables me to do exactly that–as I for a few minutes pause, reflect and listen for God's whisper.

Jesus himself followed the disciplines of Jewish prayer, which played a vital role in his culture. The following description is given under 'Synagogues' in the *Dictionary of Jesus and the Gospels*: 'The Jews were and are a praying people. Their Temple was named a "House of prayer" ([see] Isaiah 56:7), and the synagogues that Jesus frequented were also recognised in the ancient world as places of prayer.'[7] As theologian Scot McKnight explains, 'It would have been nearly impossible for Jesus to have been a Jew in the first century, at least a pious Jew, and not have participated in Israel's sacred rhythm of praying.'[8]

The ancient discipline of praying twice a day, at sunrise and sunset, was widely practised within Judaism. Many scholars believe that first-century Jews also prayed at noon, possibly indicated, for example, by Psalm 55:17: 'Morning, noon, and night you hear my concerns' (CEV), and Peter's rooftop lunchtime prayer in Acts 10:9.[9]

Yet, at the same time, Jesus found innovative ways of incorporating more spontaneous prayer into every aspect of life. For instance, while he appears to keep the Jewish discipline of morning prayer ('Very early the next morning, Jesus got up and went to a place where he could be alone and pray' [Mark 1:35 CEV]), we also see that his approach took him way beyond the formal disciplines of prayer. Jesus lived a life in which prayer pervaded every dimension, manifesting his own human dependence on God–even to the final hour of his suffering and the spontaneous raw honesty of his cry from the cross (see Mark 14:35–42; Luke 3:21; 5:16; 6:12–13; 9:18, 28–29; 23:34).

Which leads us to another important observation. It is easy to assume that to live a genuinely Christ-like life is to attain, somehow, a perfect and permanent state of inner peace and communion with God. But this misguided notion not only fails to reflect our experience of reality–in which distraction and suffering are part of our daily struggle–it also fails to take seriously the painful experience of Christ. Jesus' anguish in the garden of Gethsemane was the dark night of his soul as he battled with the agony of choosing God's will over his own comfort. Hours later, hanging on the cross, he cried out in the agony of both physical and spiritual pain for all to hear: 'My God, my God, where are you?' (see Matthew 27:46).

Jesus' cry of anguish from the cross is echoed by countless millions of people who suffer oppression, enslavement, abuse, disease, poverty, starvation and violence every day. 'If God is really love, then why has he abandoned me?' But while our struggles often cause us to believe that God has abandoned us, the reality is that he is always there with us, in our suffering. And this culminates with the intense pain experienced by God himself, in human form: Jesus.

Look at Psalm 22 (CEV and NIV), from which Jesus' cry 'My God, my God, where are you?' is a direct quote. It is a poem with a twist: 'Why are you so far from saving me? Won't you listen to my groans and come to my rescue? O my God, I cry out day and night, but you do not answer, and I can never rest,' the writer goes on to complain. But then, even in his pain, he acknowledges, 'Yet you are enthroned as the Holy One ... In you our fathers put their trust; they trusted and you delivered them. They cried to you and were saved; in you they trusted and were not disappointed ... I can count all my bones; people stare and gloat over me. They divide my garments among them and cast lots for my clothing. But you, O LORD, be not far off; O my Strength, come quickly to help me ... You who fear the LORD, praise him! For he has not despised or disdained the suffering of the afflicted one; he has not hidden his face from him but has listened to his cry for help.'

Following Christ does not bring an escape from pain, complexity or doubt–nor does it ensure a constant sense of God's closeness. Ours will sometimes be the experience of isolation and aloneness that even Christ felt. But, even in his darkest and most disturbed moments, Christ reminded himself that beyond the horizon of his feelings and emotions is a greater truth–'he has not despised or disdained the suffering of the afflicted one; he has not hidden his face from him but has listened to his cry for help' (Psalm 22:24).

God is there–even at the cross. And so it is that even in the desolation of this moment, perhaps through the remembrance and recital of the famous psalm, Christ recognises and clings to God's presence, as is demonstrated by his cry: 'Father, forgive them, for they do not know what they are doing' (Luke 23:34). And, finally, in words of peaceful surrender and extraordinary intimacy, he says: 'Father, into your hands I commit my spirit' (Luke 23:46).

A CHANGED HEART

The teacher explained to his apprentice that he was planning to leave for a few days to spend some time alone in the monastery.

'Just as a fish dies on the land and, to live again, must return to water, so I must return to solitude.'

The apprentice looked puzzled and then asked, 'Therefore, should I leave my business too and go to a monastery?'

'Certainly not!' the teacher said with a smile. 'You must hold on to your business and go back to your heart.'[10]

Developing a 'Rule of Life' is not just a tool for 'spiritual' professionals; it is equally vital for ordinary people with jobs, college assignments or kids to feed. In fact, developing discipline can be even more essential for those who are trying to make sense of Christ's call to apprenticeship in the middle of a busy and demanding daily schedule. Richard Foster, in his book *Celebration of Discipline*, describes it this way:

> God intends the disciplines of the spiritual life to be for ordinary human beings: people who have jobs, who care for children, who must wash dishes and mow lawns. In fact, the Disciplines are best exercised in the midst of our normal activities. If they are to have a transforming effect, the effect must be found in the ordinary junctures of human life.[11]

There are those who delight in telling us that it is impossible to hear God's voice in the midst of the busyness of our lives–and that his voice can only be heard when we consciously retreat from 'the world'. Just as it is impossible to be thrown into a furnace and remain cool, they say, so it is impossible to find peace in the heat and pace of everyday life.

But true peace does not come from the outside, but from the inside; it stems from the quality of our inner life and our relationship with God.

Peace can be found in any circumstance, regardless of the pace of life.

Woven even into the turbulent fabric of our hectic lives is structure and a routine. We all live with routines, rituals and regimes of one sort or another (even though we may not think of them as forming a rule). How many people start the day with a coffee, ten minutes of radio or TV news and a quick check of their email and mobile phone inboxes, followed by the newspaper or a chapter of a novel on the train or the bus as it carries them to work. And what about those health and fitness routines: healthy eating and regular exercise for a healthy heart or the beauty regime for that perfect skin.

Developing a spiritual routine is therefore more about adapting or adjusting our existing rituals than finding a completely new pattern of life. Rather than attempting to adopt an intimidating set of new rules, which we are bound to be unable to keep, it is better to begin by incorporating simple changes into our existing daily regime. As Dietrich Bonhoeffer wrote:

> There is not one of us who lives so hectic a life that he cannot spare ten minutes a day–morning or evening–letting himself be still and quieting all around him. Let eternity alone be in your thoughts and in its light question yourself ... let the mind go free and the soul find its way into the Father's house, returning home to find rest.[12]

The key is to start small so that our chosen spiritual disciplines become a natural part of our daily routine, rather than an unrealistic striving to achieve too much too soon—which is almost guaranteed to lead us to give up altogether.

However, it is also crucial to understand that unless we are intentional and deliberate, unless we give some thought and energy to how we will keep developing as apprentices of Jesus, we will not progress. Anyone who has tried to pray or meditate will know, only too well, that strange inner resistance to free ourselves from the noises and distractions which surround us. So strong is this pull, especially when we first try to be still, that it is only through the discipline of perseverance that we can find the silence we so hungrily seek.

The task of every apprentice of Christ is to develop rituals around the ordinary, to find ways of developing spiritual rituals in unexpected ways—small habits, practices and disciplines that transform ordinary events. However, a Rule of Life needs to fit you well—it needs to be bespoke—so that it suits your circumstances and personality, or it will soon become a heavy burden and be discarded. Indeed, many of the difficulties people have with prayer are unnecessary. They are often caused when we attempt to adopt models of devotion which are suited to somebody else's temperament rather than our own.

Any routine we adopt should always be flexible. It should change and evolve as our circumstances and needs change and evolve. And, if the commitments we've made are just not practical or doable, we need to revise them.

In the monastic tradition, when novices first draw up their own Rule of Life, invariably they feel it necessary to demonstrate their commitment by making their disciplines as demanding as possible, only to become disheartened and disillusioned when they cannot maintain such a burdensome 'yoke'. The older monks have learnt that it is better to have disciplines that are not harsh and which can therefore be sustained with joy. Corrinne Ware emphasises this in her book *Saint Benedict on the Freeway* with:

> One thing the past has taught us is that when discipline loses the heartfelt spirit that gave rise to it in the first place, that discipline becomes a tyranny. When 'I yearn' becomes 'I have to,' something dies.[13]

Looked at this way, creating enough space to listen to God's whisper need not be a daunting experience but something which is achievable and, ultimately, liberating.

So it is that, through the steady development of the rhythm of a personalised spiritual routine, those who choose to follow Christ–to apprentice themselves to him–learn to listen to the quiet 'whisper' which is the voice of God.

'Lord, here is my prayer. Make me your servant.'

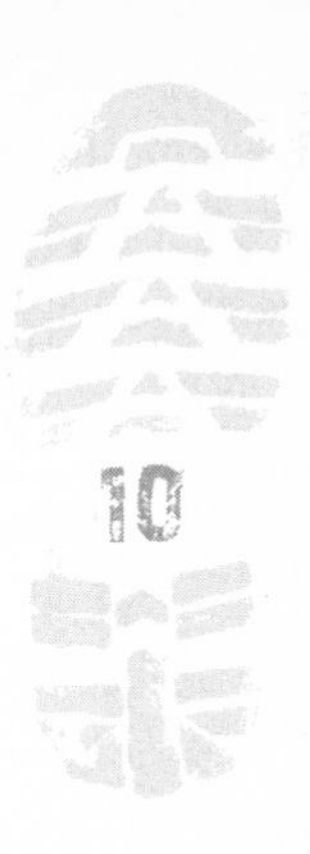

ENGAGING

Once upon a time, on a small planet in a small solar system on the rim of a large galaxy, a child was born.

The child grew to become the founder of a new way of life. He began his life of public service by proclaiming that the spirit of the Creator was upon him, inspiring him to proclaim the good news of liberation to the poor, the oppressed and the enslaved.

However, over the following centuries, this new way of life became a religion, and this religion grew and became the most prosperous religion in the world. Its leading adherents became rich and powerful, often through the oppression and enslavement of the very kind of people their founder had come to liberate.

During this time, many of the adherents of this religion developed a complex bubble of subculture in which they lived and celebrated their beliefs and blessings without having to remember the poor, the oppressed and the enslaved outside the bubble.

As the generations passed, the adherents of this religion gradually lost sight of the meaning of the message of their founder because, after all, that message was irrelevant to their new reality: it was largely concerned with the world beyond their cultural bubble. They had no idea that their understanding of the message was skewed because, of course, everything within the bubble reinforced their distorted version of the message.

Then it happened. A small group of bubble dwellers, those who occasionally had the opportunity to travel outside, began to realise that there was a problem. In the world outside the membrane, they saw firsthand the kinds of oppression and poverty to which the founder of the way had addressed himself. One by one they began to realise that the bubble was actually a prison, a false kingdom from which they needed to escape in order to be reconnected with the original message and mission of their founder.

Some of these dissenters began to speak openly about the tension they felt between the bubble world and the real world of poverty beyond the membrane. They began to call on the Creator to save them from the bubble and grant them the courage to cross over the boundary that divided them from the outside world. And they encouraged others to join them as they began to break the silence, pierce the membrane and let a new future flow.[1]

The philosopher René Descartes, who coined the famous phrase 'I think, therefore I am,' summed up the intellectual priorities of the West when he emphasised that it was 'intuition and deduction, on which alone ... we must rely in the acquisition of knowledge.'[2]

But this championing of reason above all else has left us with a cultural hangover: we have turned spiritual maturity into a matter of 'what you know' rather than 'what you *do* about what you know.'

The majority of Christians today have come to learn about Christ and what it means to follow him via a learning environment based around sermons, Bible studies, books, conferences and seminars. We 'study the Word' alone and with friends, and on Sundays we listen to preachers who have 'studied' it in more depth than we have.

Of course, Bible study has its place, but in the experience of Jesus' first apprentices, there was so much more to their multi-dimensional, life-long journey with Christ.

The modern notion of 'study' conjures up images of students spending hours bent over large dusty tomes in badly lit libraries, trying to absorb information well enough to pass an exam. But little of what we 'study' in this way is of real value for the challenges and vagaries of life.

LEARNING FROM JESUS

Many of us view study as nothing more than a necessary evil, one that has to be endured in order to attain the knowledge we need to succeed. And while some would say that all study has an intrinsic value, even if we don't always see it, my experience is that this is one of those statements most often made by learners who somehow avoided being crushed by their studies. They are the exception, not the norm. The terms 'disciple', 'follower' and 'apprentice' suggest a vital, multi-faceted learning that our actual practice of 'study' normally lacks.

Jesus' original apprentices, as we've seen, benefited from a learning style of breadth and depth, variety and diversity. Charles F. Melchert, in his book *Wise Teaching*, explains what apprentices learn:

> If a disciple is an apprentice, then the teacher is the master not just of texts and sayings but of the practices that are learned, not so much by reading about them, but by engaging in them ... Apprentice learning requires observation, imitation, trial and error, learning from mistakes, formation of habits and skills, reflection on why things happened as they did and what could be done differently next time.[3]

Jesus knew that allowing others to learn for themselves was the best way of getting his apprentices to come to a real understanding of the teaching of Scripture and its implications for their lives. When a person is enabled to learn in this way, to arrive at understanding under their own steam and in their own way, not only is the learning deeper and permanent, the learner's self-esteem and self-worth are developed too. Melchert goes on to explain:

> Apprentices listen and watch a master, then are given small tasks to develop skills and understandings of their own. They are gradually given greater responsibilities and opportunities to try out for themselves. Then they review their experiences with the master for evaluation and further instruction.[4]

Within the rabbinic model, an apprentice learns in dialogue with their teacher and with other apprentices. This is an active process. It involves practice, making mistakes and experiencing both failure and success. There are times of reflection, debate and questioning. There will be periods of theorising: reaching conclusions, forming ideas and principles that summarise what has been learned. And there is a pragmatic side to learning, practising what has been learned based on the understanding gained thus far. The process of learning is a cycle: continued practice–living out the teachings of the master–leads to further mistakes and setbacks and fresh opportunities for learning.

TRIAL AND ERROR

We see a wonderful picture of this kind of active learning method demonstrated in chapter 9 of Luke's gospel, when Jesus gathers his closest apprentices and sends the twelve of them out, in groups of two, into the towns and villages around Galilee to introduce people to his new ideas about the kingdom of God.

Luke gives us a fascinating account of the way that Jesus gives responsibility to his apprentices. In their enthusiasm, the apprentices seem to get it–and then they don't. They understand, but they are still learning. Luke shows how they are given the opportunity to learn as much from their mistakes as from their successes. Jesus gives his apprentices the room to experiment, fail and learn from their experience.

When the disciples return from their travels, they share with Jesus what they have experienced (Luke 9:10). After this, Jesus probes them a little deeper; he questions them about his true identity (Luke 9:18). Only Peter–perhaps Jesus' most outspoken follower–comes up with the right answer: 'The Messiah' (Luke 9:20 CEV). But even though he answers correctly, Peter goes on to misunderstand his own answer–and does not fully grasp the implications of his new-found understanding (see Matthew 16:21–23).

Despite their apparent failure to understand (reinforced in Luke 9:46 by a subsequent squabble over which one of them would be the best), Luke astonishes us with the opening sentence of his next chapter: 'After this the Lord appointed *seventy-two* others and sent them two by two ahead of him to every town and place where he was about to go' (Luke 10:1, emphasis added). Not only does Jesus continue to entrust his apprentices with great responsibility–he significantly expands the project!

Trying to protect learners from the pain of failure and mistakes only keeps them from learning. Active learning is challenging, but if learners do not actually engage with what they are learning, they remain dependent on the teacher. Their education will be stunted and shallow, and they remain susceptible to manipulation and control by others. Ecclesiastes 12:12 (CEV) even includes a warning about the manipulation of information, via extraneous ideas tacked onto the nitty-gritty of God's message:

> There is no end to books, and too much study will wear you out.

ACTIVE LEARNING

We learn ...

> 10 percent of what we read.
> 20 percent of what we hear.
> 30 percent of what we see.
> 50 percent of what we see and hear.
> 70 percent of what we say.
> 90 percent of what we say and do.[5]

If our learning experiences only involve listening and reading, then we will never fulfil our learning potential. Passive learning fails to stimulate our senses to the point where we actually integrate what we know into our lives, combining what we are learning with what we have already learned so that it sinks in and becomes a part of our life. We must *do* something with knowledge for it to become part of who we are. 'We learn best when we "do" something with information–when we use it, when it ceases to be a passive experience and we actively engage with the text.'[6]

Consider how you learned to ride a bike or use a computer. You were actively involved. You took risks. You experienced the consequences of your actions–both successes and failures. You then chose either to continue with what you were doing or to take a new and different action. What allowed you to master the new skill was your active participation in the event and the time you spent reflecting on it. Experience accompanied by reflection taught you more than any manual or lecture ever could.

Genuine learning always requires that we keep moving forward–beyond our comfort zones. As long as we have breath, we continue to learn. Indeed, as apprentices of Jesus Christ, we never truly finish learning because we will always be striving to live out our goal of 'imitating Christ'.

Apprenticeship, then, doesn't necessarily require great academic ability–just the ability to engage in life, reflect on your actions, draw conclusions and then put them into further action. It's an ongoing process of living, reflecting, understanding and taking action.

THE SPIRITUAL LIFE

Far from offering us a 'whole life' experience, our twenty-first-century Western culture has compartmentalised spirituality. Our spiritual 'side' is regarded as something 'a little aside' from the rest of our life. Spirituality is relegated to the fringes. However, surprisingly, the Hebrew Scriptures contain no word for 'spiritual' and, more astonishing yet, Jesus never used the phrase 'spiritual life'. The reason for this is simple: for Jesus, the *whole of life* was spiritual.

Eugene Peterson says: 'Spirituality is not immaterial as opposed to material; not interior as opposed to exterior; not invisible as opposed to visible. Quite the contrary; spirituality has much to do with the material, the external, and the visible. What it properly conveys is living as opposed to dead.'[7]

Gordon Mursell, in *Christian Spirituality*, writes:

> Hebrew knows no absolute distinction between the physical, material world, and a wholly separate 'spiritual' world. The two are inextricably linked.[8]

The life of the Hebrews was earthy. Reality was not an abstract, theoretical or academic idea to be contemplated; rather it was something to be experienced, embraced and worked at. God was not an absent or abstruse philosophical idea; nor was knowledge of God primarily accessed by the intellect. In fact, the Hebrews had no word that corresponds exactly to our modern understanding of 'intellect' or 'intellectual'.

We get a sense of this by looking at the definition of the Hebrew verb *yada*. *Yada* means 'to know': to encounter and experience something or someone in a personal way. *Yada* is not disembodied knowledge. It cannot be obtained and possessed by standing back from life. It requires ongoing, active, intentional engagement. Knowledge is productive and creative; it is more than information, more than theory. Knowing, in this sense, demands a response in the practical domain of behaviour. Adam 'knew' Eve! *Yada* insists that true knowledge of God can never simply be obtained through intellectual understanding.

> Josiah ... always did right–he gave justice to the poor and was honest. That's what it means to truly know me.
>
> Jeremiah 22:15–16 (CEV)

Biblical spirituality knows no divorce or separation between the seemingly mundane and the more formal religious practices. Administration and legislation were part of worship. Tending the soil, caring for the animals, harvesting the crops and sustaining the relationships of the community were acts of thankfulness and worship to God.

The Hebrew Scriptures weren't written with the intention of being a devotional manual to provide inspiration in those 'special' moments. They were written to record and remember God's ongoing involvement in the life of his people. When we forget this context, we might be tempted to wonder why we have book after book in the Old Testament devoted to apparently tedious laws and boring bureaucracy. Yet while we may separate the ordering of life and business from our spirituality, the Hebrews recognised that all of life belongs to God.

For instance, consider the laws, statutes and ordinances of the book of Leviticus. Throughout Leviticus, we find a wide range of practices and instructions: from healthy eating to family affairs, from medical advice to farming instructions, from correct religious protocol to international relations. Leviticus chapter 19, for instance, is a comprehensive vision of holiness that embraces every aspect of individual and corporate life, from guidance on the breeding of cattle to respect for parents, instructions about the harvesting of crops to principles about hiring workers, caring for refugees and the use of accurate weights in trading.

If you could travel back in a time capsule and ask the Hebrews how they found time for their 'spiritual life' with all of this creation-tending legislation to contend with, they would probably look at you a little confused. All of these things *were* part of what it meant to be spiritual. The segmented nature of modern life did not exist. Spirituality infused every area of life.

Our lives do not have a separate 'spiritual section', like you might find in your local bookstore. If our life is the whole shop, then *all* of it is spiritual!

But none of this is to suggest that meditation, contemplation and other spiritual disciplines do not have their place in our development as Christ's apprentices. The problem is that somehow, in the very process of affirming and valuing these practices as spiritual, we too often turn our backs on a greater truth. We forget that *all* of life is a spiritual experience–a way of knowing and experiencing God–and can and should, therefore, form part of our spiritual development.

ACTIVE SPIRITUALITY

On the many occasions when the people of Israel got overfocused on the *religious* or *spiritual* dimensions of life, turning them into lifeless traditions, God spoke through his prophets and criticised them for their preoccupation with empty words, songs and religious festivals. Through the prophets, God called for deeds of mercy and justice in public life. See, for example, Isaiah 1:10–20; 58. The book of Amos includes the following:

> *I hate, I despise your religious feasts;*
> *I cannot stand your assemblies.*
> *Even though you bring me burnt offerings and*
> *grain offerings,*
> *I will not accept them.*
> *Though you bring choice fellowship offerings,*

I will have no regard for them.
Away with the noise of your songs!
I will not listen to the music of your harps.
But let justice roll on like a river,
righteousness like a never-failing stream!

Amos 5:21–24

The problem, of course, was not that fasting, praying and worship were inherently wrong. The problem was that issues of injustice and oppression were being ignored. The blessings the people sought would only be forthcoming if they put their house in order and focused their attention on the more 'mundane' issues of life–serving their neighbours and becoming advocates of the poor and oppressed.

> The Lord God has told us what is right and what he demands: 'See that justice is done, let mercy be your first concern, and humbly obey your God.'
>
> MICAH 6:8 CEV

Søren Kierkegaard, the Danish philosopher, grew up in the countryside surrounded by farms where geese were raised. Each spring he would watch as a new gaggle of goslings was hatched, fed and fattened for the table.

Over the course of their short lives, these geese would regularly gorge themselves at continually refilled troughs of grain until they were so fat they could hardly walk. Kierkegaard imagined that the geese probably believed their lives to be perfect. Every need they had was catered for in abundance.

When autumn came, the *wild* geese that had spent the warm summer months in Denmark would gather in preparation for their southerly migration. As these geese assembled to fly south, they would circle in the skies above the farms, calling out to the farm geese to join in their flight.

The farm geese would lift their heads from the feeding trough and look up into the skies and listen to the call of their wild cousins. For the first time in their lives, they would become animated and begin running, as best they could, around their enclosure. They would attempt, with all the energy they could muster, to fly. But their gluttonous diet and life of luxury meant that they had grown far too fat to become airborne.

And then, just as quickly as the commotion had started, the wild geese would be gone. The fattened farm geese would watch them briefly, put their heads back down, and return to their grain, slowly eating themselves to death.

The symbol for the Holy Spirit–the Spirit of Christ–adopted by the ancient Celtic Church was that of a wild goose. Christ's apprentices are called to raise their heads from their feeding troughs, spread wings of faith and live out a spirituality centred on their love for God and for others.

Love God. Love your neighbour as yourself. Nothing else matters.

INTIMACY AND INVOLVEMENT

With all our talk about Christ-centred spirituality, we still have a problem. In the English language, the word *spirituality* has become far too limited in its connotations. Nowadays, whenever we speak of 'spirituality', we end up talking and thinking in compartmentalised ways. We lack an adequate word to express what we really want to say.

As a result, we allow our culture to define our understanding of spirituality and come to assume that the limited horizon represented by most definitions of 'spirituality' is all there is on offer. As Lesslie Newbigin once wrote, 'Every human society is governed by assumptions, normally taken for granted ... There is no such thing as an ideological vacuum'.[9] We *assume* an understanding of spirituality that is inherently unbiblical and which lacks the breadth and depth we need to grow in our experience and knowledge of God.

A new word is needed – a word that expresses an 'integrated' spirituality, a term for authentic Christ-centred spirituality that doesn't require constant unpacking. Perhaps the best way to express this type of spirituality is through the phrase 'intimacy and involvement'. *Intimacy* refers to the vertical aspect of our spirituality, the development of our relationship with God through honesty, openness and trust. *Involvement* refers to the horizontal aspect of our spirituality – the natural outflow of that relationship into all other areas of life.

Once we have established this holistic understanding, we have to remind ourselves that, in the teachings of Jesus, intimacy and involvement are always organically connected. They are two interconnected categories. The combination is vital. Having one without the other is like attempting to run a marathon on one leg.

Those who subscribe to an 'otherworldly' notion of the Christian faith, concerned only with the inner life, as well as those who focus exclusively on activism and public service, end up abandoning biblically rooted Christian spirituality.

Talk about the inner *versus* the outer life is always an attempt to drive a wedge between two things which are, in essence, unified. This ends up producing a perilous and destructive dualism that rejects the teaching of both the Old and New Testaments.

Authentic Christian faith requires us to be *with* God *for* other people, and *with* other people *for* God. We must find the equilibrium between intimacy and involvement. As Archbishop Rowan Williams has argued, 'A religious life is a material life ... a fundamental mistake is to consider belief itself ... as more or less exclusively a mental event.'[10]

In many cases, a spirituality that is solely focused on the inner life becomes dead and lifeless. For the most part, it falls foul of the criticisms which Freud and others have made of religion–that it is no more than a crutch for the weak. Mission, activism and public service which are detached from an inner spirituality will ultimately prove to be bankrupt of transformational power and energy. Either way, our faith becomes impotent and sterile. Genuine Christian spirituality is lost and a light that should shine in the darkness and bring hope to the world is extinguished.

The Bible consistently contradicts the imagined divide between the sacred and the secular, calling instead for faith and action to function in harmony with one another. The Hebrew word for 'faith' also implies 'faithfulness', i.e. obedient activity. The connection between right beliefs and right actions is made explicit by Jesus himself in his famous parable of the sheep and the goats when he concludes: 'Whatever you did for one of the least of these ... you did for me' (Matthew 25:40).[11]

> This is a large work I've called you into, but don't be overwhelmed by it. It's best to start small. Give a cool cup of water to someone who is thirsty, for instance. The smallest act of giving or receiving makes you a true apprentice.
>
> MATTHEW 10:41–42 THE MESSAGE

As Lesslie Newbigin points out: 'If we turn to the Gospels we are bound to note the indissoluble nexus between deeds and words.'[12] Or, to put it even more bluntly (as one of Jesus' first apprentices, James, does): 'Faith, if it has no works, is dead' (James 2:17 NASB). Michael Riddell, in his book *The Sacred Journey*, describes it this way:

> When the inner life becomes detached from the outer life, it easily descends into narcissism. The word 'integrity' indicates wholeness, and to achieve it requires a balance and harmony between public and private life. That which we claim to be aware of in our souls must become visible before it is credible. Likewise, our actions need to spring from the depths of our spirit if they are to be of substance and significance.[13]

Jesus' final words to his apprentices, as recorded by Matthew, are: '*Go* ... and surely I am with you always' (Matthew 28:19–20). Integrated within the thinking of Christ are these twin principles of intimacy and involvement. As far as he is concerned, the 'stay-at-home church' can never experience the depth of intimacy it so craves, for it is also in the act of 'going' out into the world that we encounter his presence, often in new and different ways. As one broadcaster put it, 'If you really want a religious experience–go and feed the poor.'[14]

It intrigued the apprentices to see their teacher disappear for a few hours each week on the evening of the Sabbath.

They suspected that he was secretly meeting with the Almighty, so they chose one of their number to follow him and report back.

On the evening of the next Sabbath, the eager apprentice followed his teacher at a distance, hidden by the shadows so as not to be seen.

He watched as his teacher disguised himself in peasant clothes, visited the cottage of an elderly paralysed woman, cleaned her home and prepared a Sabbath meal for her.

When the spy got back, the other apprentices asked, 'Where did the teacher go? Did he ascend into heaven?'

'No,' came the response, 'he went even higher.'

Intimacy with God and involvement with society are inseparably connected. True intimacy with God is the outcome of our involvement in his world; and involvement in God's world is the outcome of genuine intimacy with him. They belong inseparably together. To ignore one is always to destroy the quality and depth of the other.

BECOMING APPRENTICES

'The world doesn't need more words, not even more "right" words,' argues John Hayes, head of InnerCHANGE, a monastic ministry. 'The world needs more words made flesh. The world needs more people to live the good news incarnationally, in a way that can been seen, heard and handled.'[15]

Living in the great turbulence of El Salvador in the 1970s, Archbishop Oscar Romero was a man who knew what it meant to live as Christ's apprentice in times of intense darkness. He was a leader of great courage who witnessed sweeping social change, and he ultimately paid with his life for his determination to speak the truth on behalf of his people. In a talk given to a gathering of local churches, he spoke of their role in bringing in the kingdom of God:

> It helps, now and then, to step back and take the long view. The Kingdom is not only beyond our efforts, it is even beyond our vision. We accomplish in our lifetime only a tiny fraction of the magnificent enterprise that is God's work ... We water seeds already planted, knowing that they hold future promise. We lay foundations that will need further development. We provide yeast that produces effects far beyond our capabilities. We cannot do everything, and there is a sense of liberation in realising that. This enables us to do something, and to do it very well. It may not be complete, but it is a beginning, a step along the way, an opportunity for the Lord's grace to enter

> and do the rest. We may never see the end results, but that is the difference between the master builder and the worker. We are workers, not master builders; ministers not messiahs. We are prophets of a future not our own.[16]

The courage and vision epitomised by Oscar Romero are at the heart of what it means to be an apprentice of Jesus: learning to live, to serve, to move forward with love and with hope. Apprenticeship entails embracing life's sacred journey, wherever you are starting from, without fear of leaving the past behind, without fear of where you will end up.

As Jesus said in Luke 6:40, 'Everyone who is fully trained will be like his teacher'.

May God bless you with discomfort
at easy answers, half-truths, and superficial relationships
so that you may live deep within your heart.
May God bless you with anger
at injustice, oppression, and exploitation of people,
so that you may work for justice, freedom, and peace.
May God bless you with tears
to shed for those who suffer pain, rejection, hunger and war
so that you may reach out your hand to comfort them and
to turn their pain into joy.
And may God bless you with enough foolishness

to believe that you can make a difference in the world,
so that you can do what others claim cannot be done
to bring justice and kindness to all our children and the poor.
Amen.[17]

NOTES

Chapter : Acknowledgements

1. Kenneth Schmitz, cited by Stanley Hauerwas in The Peaceable Kingdom' (South Bend, Ind.: Notre Dame University Press, 1983), 27.

Chapter 1: Journeying

1. Throughout this book, the stories told are based on those I have read or heard and then re-told and adapted over the years. Where I have been able to remember or trace the source, I have credited it. But, credited or not, in each case their origins are older than I am.

2. *The Motorcycle Diaries* screenplay by José Rivera, directed by Walter Salles (Buenos Aires, Argentina: BD Cine, 2004).

3. Ibid.

4. Richard Dawkins, *River Out of Eden: A Darwinian View of Life* (New York: BasicBooks, 1995), quoted in Michael Lloyd, *Café Theology* (London: Alpha International, 2005).

5. Broadcast on the BBC *Third Programme* in 1948, see *www.bringyou.to/apologetics/p20.htm*.

6. G. W. F. Leibniz, 'The Principles of Nature and Grace, Based on Reason', *Monadologie* (1714), accessed at *http://study.abingdon.org.uk/rs/AS%20Philosophy%20notes/cosmological_argument.pdf*.

7. *www.martynjoseph.com* / *www.piperecords.co.uk/martyn/resource/mjlyrics.pdf*. Used with permission.

8. Theology: from *theos*, the Greek word for 'God', and *logos*, the Greek word for 'words'.

9. Erwin Raphael McManus, *Soul Cravings* (Nashville: Nelson, 2006), entry 3.

10. Jesuit philosopher Anthony de Mello, *www.demello.org*.

11. Etymology: Hebrew *rabbi*, 'my master', from *rabh* 'master' and the suffix for 'my'.

12. The Hebrew word for a follower of a rabbi is *talmid* (*talmidim*, plural), which is usually translated as 'disciple', but which more accurately and graphically refers to 'one being apprenticed'.

13. Charles F. Melchert, *Wise Teaching* (Harrisburg, Penn.: Trinity Press International, 1998), 278–79.

14. The Mishnah is a collection of the oral traditions taught by the rabbis. It was organised and compiled about 200 AD by R. Judah ha-Nasi I and has since undergone numerous changes. It includes the civil laws of Judaism as well as the teachings of the first five books of the Old Testament. It is included in the first part of the Talmud.

15. *Avot 1:4* [Ethics of the Fathers] chapter 1, in Mishnah 4.

16. The term *kingdom of God* means 'kingship' or 'ruler-ship' of God in the here and now, the nitty-gritty of everyday life–it was not a reference, as is now commonly assumed, to some otherworldly existence after death. For an in-depth discussion of this, read my book *The Lost Message of Jesus* (Grand Rapids.: Zondervan, 2003).

17. Matthew chooses to use the phrase the 'kingdom of heaven', rather than 'kingdom of God' as used by the other three gospel writers. This is because his original audience was largely made up of devout Jews who, out of reverence, would not directly use the name of God. So Matthew replaces 'God' with 'heaven'.

18. A story, based on Jesus' famous parable, that I heard told, as a teenager, by a Brazilian preacher named Juan Carlos Ortiz.

19. Ted Hughes, in a letter to his son Nicholas, undated 1986, printed in *The Daily Telegraph*, *www.telegraph.co.uk/arts/main.jhtml?xml=/arts/2007/10/08/nosplit/boted108.xml.*

Chapter 2: Longing

1. Ronald Rolheiser, *Against an Infinite Horizon* (London: Hodder & Stoughton, 1995).

2. Erwin Raphael McManus, *Soul Cravings* (Nashville: Nelson, 2006).

3. Rolheiser, *Infinite Horizon*.

4. From Michael Foreman's classic children's story *Dinosaurs and All That Rubbish* (London: Puffin Books, 1974). With permission.

5. Traditional tale, first heard by the author in an American bar.

6. Alex Garland, *The Beach* (New York: Riverhead, 1997).

7. Esther de Waal, *A Life-Giving Way: A Commentary on the Rule of St. Benedict* (Collegeville, Minn.: Liturgical Press, 1995), 17.

8. Discipline, in *The Oxford Pocket Dictionary of Current English* (Oxford: Oxford University Press, 2008).

9. From C. G. Jung's essay 'The Stages of Life', *Collected Works of C. G. Jung*, vol. 8 (Princeton, N.J.: Princeton University Press, 1967).

10. Ibid.

11. M. Scott Peck, *The Road Less Travelled: A New Psychology of Love, Traditional Values and Spiritual Growth* (New York: Touchstone, 1998), 2.

12. Dietrich Bonhoeffer, Psalm 119 in *Meditations on Psalms*, Edwin Robertson, ed. and trans. (Grand Rapids: Zondervan, 2002), 94.

13. *creatingminds.org/quotes/passion.htm.*

14. Or 'Don't waste your energy striving for perishable food ... Work for the food that sticks with you, food that nourishes your lasting life' (John 6:27, The Message).

Chapter 3: Believing

1. Widely attributed to German philosopher and writer Friedrich Nietzsche (1844–1900).

2. Friedrich Nietzsche, *The Gay Science* (New York: Random House, 1974).

3. Friedrich Nietzsche, *Thus Spake Zarathustra* (New York: Dover, 2000).

4. Fyodor Dostoyevsky, quoted in Nietzsche, *Zarathustra*.

5. Howard Peskett and Vinoth Ramachandra, *The Message of Missions*, (Nottingham, UK: IVP, 2003) citing Václav Havel's address to the Canadian Senate and the House of Commons in Ottawa, 29 April 1999, 'Kosovo and the end of the Nation State,' *The New York Review of Books*, 10 June 1999.

6. Jean Rostan, quoted in C. Everett Koop, *The Right to Live, the Right to Die* (Carol Stream, Ill.: Tyndale, 1976).

7. *Imago Dei* is Latin for 'image of God' and has come to be used as the theological term to denote the nature of the relationship between God and humanity.

8. Brennan Manning, *Ruthless Trust* (London: SPCK, 1992), 5.

9. Widely accredited to Marcel Proust (1871–1922), French novelist, essayist and critic.

10. Adapted from the writings of Jesuit priest Anthony de Mello, *www.demello.org*.

11. Jim Wallis, *The Soul of Politics* (New York: Orbis, 1994), 196.

12. Adapted from the writings of Jesuit priest Anthony de Mello, *www.demello.org*.

Chapter 4: Questioning

1. Adapted from Fyodor Dostoyevsky, *The Brothers Karamazov* (New York: Penguin Classics, 2003).

2. Søren Kierkegaard, *Concluding Unscientific Postscript to Philosophical Fragments*, translated by David Swenson and Walter Lowrie (Princeton, N.J.: Princeton University Press, 1941).

3. Emily Dickinson (1830–1886), 'The World Is Not Conclusion', accessed at *www.eliteskills.com/analysis_poetry/This_World_is_not_Conclusion_by_Emily_Dickinson_analysis.php*.

4. F. O'Conner, *The Habit of Being*, quoted in K. J. Clark, *When Faith Is Not Enough* (Grand Rapids: Eerdmans, 1994).

5. Woody Allen, accessed at *http://quotationsbook.com/quote/36468/*.

6. BBC Two, 'The Monastery', produced by Tiger Aspect Productions Limited, first broadcast by BBC in the UK from April 2005, broadcast 4 April 2005, accessed at *www.bbc.co.uk/pressoffice/pressreleases/stories/2005/04_april/22/monastery.shtml*, and *http://www.bbc.co.uk/pressoffice/pressreleases/stories/2005/04_april/22/monastery.shtml www.tigeraspect.co.uk/prog.asp?id=192*.

7. Cardinal Basil Hume, *The Mystery of Love* (London: Darton, Longman & Todd, 2000), 7.

8. Naquib Mahfouz, accessed at *www.worldofquotes.com/author/Naguib-Mahfouz/1/index.html*.

9. David Bowie, 'Word on a Wing', *Station to Station* album (New York: RCA Records, 1976).

10. Francis Bacon lived at a spiritually and politically tumultuous time in history, between 1561 and 1626.

11. Cardinal Basil Hume, *The Mystery of Love*, 7.

12. Attributed to Irish playwright George Bernard Shaw (1856–1950).

13. Emile Durkheim, *The Elementary Forms of Religious Life* (New York: Oxford University Press, 2008).

14. Adapted from N. T. Wright, *The Challenge of Jesus: Rediscovering Who Jesus Was and Is* (Downers Grove, Ill.: InterVarsity, 1999).

15. Adapted from the writings of Jesuit priest Anthony de Mello, *www.demello.org*.

16. Widely attributed to Indira Gandhi, prime minister of India for three terms (1966 to 1977) and for a fourth term from 1980 until her assassination in 1984.

17. William Temple (1881–1944) was the ninety-eighth archbishop of Canterbury, from 1942 until his death two years later.

18. Charles F. Melchert, *Wise Teaching: Biblical Wisdom and Educational Ministry* (London: Continuum, 1998), 10.

19. Sophia Lyon Fahs (1876–1978), *www.wisdomquotes.com.*

20. Charles M. Schulz (1922–2000). *www.quotationspage.com.*

21. Attributed to Albert Einstein, *thinkexist.com.*

Chapter 5: Belonging

1. Based on Alex Garland, *The Beach* (London: Penguin, 1997). Used with permission.

2. Henri J. M. Nouwen, *Reaching Out: The Three Movements of the Spiritual Life* (New York: Image, 1975).

3. Mother Teresa, *www.brainyquote.com.*

4. Widely attributed to Albert Schweitzer (1875–1965), theologian, musician, philosopher and physician, who received the 1952 Nobel Peace Prize in 1953 for his 1936 article 'The Ethics of Reverence for Life'.

5. Michael Riddell, *The Sacred Journey: Reflections on a Life Wholly Lived* (Oxford: Lion, 2000).

6. Based on Nick Hornby, *About a Boy* (London: Penguin, 2000). Used with permission.

7. John Ruskin (1819–1900) was an influential art critic, writer, social critic, poet and artist. *famouspoetsandpoems.com/poets/john_ruskin/quotes.*

8. The Torah comprises the first five books of the Bible, also known as the Pentateuch, namely: Genesis, Exodus, Leviticus, Numbers and Deuteronomy.

9. From the Nicene-Constantinopolitan Creed (381 AD), the most widely accepted creed in the Christian Church. Since its original formulation, it continues to be used in the Eastern Orthodox, Oriental Orthodox, Assyrian, Roman Catholic, Anglican and most Protestant churches; accessed at *www.iclnet.org/pub/resources/text/history/creed.nicene.txt.*

10. Derek Tidball, *The Message of the Cross* (Leicester, UK: IVP, 2001).

11. Stanley J. Grenz, *The Social God and the Relational Self: A Trinitarian Theology of the Imago Dei* (Louisville: Westminster John Knox Press, 2001).

12. Colin E. Gunton, *The Christian Faith: An Introduction to Christian Doctrine* (Oxford: Blackwell, 2002).

13. *The Story of Christian Spirituality*, Gordon Mursell, ed., (Oxford: Lion, 2001).

14. John Donne, 'Meditation XVII,' *Devotions Upon Emergent Occasions and Death's Duel.*

15. C. S. Lewis, 'Charity' in *The Four Loves* (New York: HarperCollins, 1960).

16. Pope Benedict, see also Miroslav Volf, 'After Our Likeness: The Church as the Image of the Trinity', 173.

17. C. S. Lewis, 'Charity', *The Four Loves*, 147.

18. Willard W. Waller, *On the Family, Education and War*, 'The Rating and Dating Complex' (Chicago: University of Chicago Press, 1938), 179.

19. Widely attributed to Ralph Waldo Emerson (1803–1882), an American essayist, philosopher, poet and orator.

Chapter 6: Serving

1. Adapted from the writings of Jesuit priest Anthony de Mello, *www.demello.org*.

2. Malvina Reynolds, written c. 1949.

3. Charles Dickens, *A Christmas Carol* (London: Bradbury and Evans, 1858), 2; accessed at *http://books.google.com.*

4. Mike Starkey, *Born to Shop* (Atlanta: Monarch, 1989), 15; long out of print but worth reading if you can get your hands on a copy.

5. Adapted from Michael Riddell, *The Sacred Journey*, 91.

6. Henri J. M. Nouwen, *Show Me the Way* (London: Darton, Longman & Todd, 1993), 38.

7. N. T. Wright, 'The God Who Raises the Dead', *Following Jesus* (London: SPCK, 1994), 61.

8. Leonardo Boff, *Jesus Christ Liberator: A Critical Christology for Our Time*, Patrick Hughes, trans. (Maryknoll, N.Y.: Orbis, 1978), 27.

9. Ruth B. Edwards, 'The Christological Basis of the Johannine Footwashing' in *Jesus of Nazareth Lord and Christ* (Grand Rapids: Eerdmans, 1994), 368–69.

10. Benjamin Franklin, *Poor Richard's Almanack*, published from 1732 to 1758; quote accessed at *www.uh.edu/engines/epi1611.htm.*

11. Mother Teresa, quoted in Daniel P. Cronin, *Through the Year with Words of Wisdom*, (Slough: St Paul Publications, 1988), 91.

12. Adapted from Pete Greig, *The Vision and the Vow: Re-Discovering Life and Grace* (Orlando: Relevant, 2004).

13. Václav Havel, playwright and Czech president 1989–1992, *thinkexist.com*

14. *salt.claretianpubs.org/romero/romero.html.*

Chapter 7: Persevering

1. Martin Luther King Jr, 'A Knock at Midnight', *Strength to Love* (New York: Harper & Row, 1963), 49–50.

2. Calvin Coolidge (1872–1933), thirtieth president of the United States (1923–1929), *www.quotationspage.com/quote/2771.html.*

3. William Shakespeare, *Hamlet* (1603). *www.william-shakespeare.info.*

4. M. Scott Peck, *The Road Less Travelled*, 12–13.

5. Jürgen Moltmann, *The Open Church: Invitation to a Messianic Life-style* (London: SCM Press, 1978), 25.

6. Eugene H. Peterson, *Christ Plays in Ten Thousand Places* (London: Hodder & Stoughton, 2005), 31.

7. Michael Lloyd, *Café Theology: Exploring Love, the Universe and Everything* (London: Alpha International, 2005).

8. C. S. Lewis, *Mere Christianity* (New York: HarperCollins, 1952).

9. Walter Wink, *The Powers That Be: Theology for a New Millennium* (New York: Bantam, 1999).

10. Gregory Boyd, *God at War* (Downers Grove, Ill.: InterVarsity, 1997).

11. Lewis, *Mere Christianity.*

12. Philip Yancey, *Where Is God When It Hurts?* (Grand Rapids: Zondervan, 1990).

13. Theodore 'Teddy' Roosevelt, 'Citizenship in a Republic', a speech given at the Sorbonne in Paris, 23 April 1910. *www.theodoreroosevelt.org/life/quotes/htm.*

14. Thomas Merton, 'The Merton Prayer', *Thoughts in Solitude* (New York: Farrar, Straus and Giroux, 1958).

15. Martin Luther King Jr, 'A Knock at Midnight', *Strength to Love,* 48–49.

Chapter 8: Forgiving

1. Christopher J. H. Wright, *Knowing Jesus through the Old Testament* (Downers Grove, Ill.: InterVarsity, 1995).

2. N. T. Wright, *Following Jesus: Biblical Reflections on Discipleship*, 'The Final Sacrifice: Hebrews' (Grand Rapids: Eerdmans, 1995), 7.

3. For an explanation of these messages, see my book *The Lost Message of Jesus* (Grand Rapids: Zondervan, 2003).

4. See the Montgomery, Alabama, Bus Boycott story in chapter 7, 'Perservering', III, from Martin Luther King Jr, *Strength to Love*, 'A Knock at Midnight' (New York: Harper & Row, 1963), 48–50.

5. A phrase probably inspired by Gandhi, who said: 'An eye for an eye makes the whole world blind', accessed at *www.quotationspage.com/quote/30302.html*; *usliberals.about.com/od/patriotactcivilrights/a/KLKWords.htm*.

6. In the last two lines, Paul is quoting from Proverbs 25:21.

7. Martin Luther King Jr., *Strength to Love*, 37.

8. Quoted in John L. Ruth, *Forgiveness: A Legacy of the West Nickel Mines Amish School* (Scottdale, Penn.: Herald Press, 2008).

9. Ruth, *Forgiveness*. Ruth chronicles the extraordinarily forgiving responses from the Amish community in Nickel Mines, Pennsylvania, after Charles Carl Roberts IV, whose first child had died, took ten girls hostage in October 2006, shot all of them (killing five), then shot himself.

10. Based on an article in *Youthworker* magazine, cited in Steve Chalke and Paul Hansford, *He Never Said*, 'An eye for an eye' (London: Hodder and Stoughton, 2000), 31–32.

11. Martin Luther King Jr, *Strength to Love*, 35.

12. C. S. Lewis, *Forgiveness* (New York: Macmillan, 1960), essay accessed at *www.oholy.net/stolga/cs_lewis.html*.

13. C. S. Lewis, essay 'On Forgiveness' (New York: Macmillan, 1960), cited in Steve Chalke and Paul Hansford, *He Never Said*, 'An eye for an eye' (London: Hodder and Soughton, 2000), 26.

14. Alexander Pope (1688–1744), 'An Essay on Criticism' (1711). *www.bartleby.com/59/3/toerrishuman.html.*

15. Gerard Kelly, 'I Choose to Forgive', *Spoken Worship: Living Words for Personal and Public Prayer* (Grand Rapids: Zondervan, 2007), 37–38. Used with permission.

Chapter 9: Listening

1. Erwin Raphael McManus, *Soul Cravings*, entry 9.

2. Martin Luther, quoted in 'Radical Empathy', a sermon by Calum I. MacLeod at Fourth Presbyterian Church, Chicago, 14 September 2008; accessed at *www.fourthchurch.org/2008archive.html*.

3. McManus, *Soul Cravings*, entry 9.

4. In 313, in the Edict of Milan, Emperor Constantine and Emperor Licinius (co-emperors of the Roman Empire, Constantine in the West and Licinius in the East) announced toleration of all religions. No longer were Christians subject to penalties for professing Christianity (under which many had been martyred). Church property that had been confiscated was returned.

5. Benedict's *Rule of Life* is the basis on which Benedictine monks form their communities.

6. Cardinal Basil Hume, *The Mystery of Love*, 50–51.

7. E. Yamauchi, 'Synagogues' in *Dictionary of Jesus and the Gospels*, Joel B. Green, Scot McKnight, I. Howard Marshall, eds. (Leicester, UK: IVP, 1992), 782.

8. Scot McKnight, *Praying With the Church: Following Jesus Daily, Hourly, Today* (Brewster, Mass.: Paraclete, 2006), 32.

9. 'The next day about noon these men were coming near Joppa. Peter went up on the roof of the house to pray' (Acts 10:9 CEV).

10. Adapted from the writings of Jesuit priest Anthony de Mello, *www.demello.org*.

11. Richard J. Foster, *Celebration of Discipline: The Path to Spiritual Growth* (San Francisco: HarperSanFrancisco, 1988).

12. Dietrich Bonhoeffer, 'Psalm 62', *Meditations on Psalms*, 31.

13. Corinne Ware, *Saint Benedict on the Freeway: A Rule of Life for the 21st Century* (Nashville: Abingdon, 2001), 60.

Chapter 10: Engaging

1. Inspired by and adapted from a story by Brian McLaren for the Delirious album *Kingdom of Comfort* (Furious/EMI, 2008). Used with permission.

2. *The Philosophical Writings of Descartes,* Vol. 1, 'Rules for the Direction of the Mind', Rule 9, translated by John Cottingham, Robert Stoothoff, Dugald Murdoch, Anthony Patrick Kenny (Cambridge University Press, 1985), 33.

3. Charles F. Melchert, *Wise Teaching*, 224.

4. Melchert, *Wise Teaching*, 252.

5. Gordon Dryden and Jeannette Vos, *The Learning Revolution: To Change the Way the World Learns* (Stafford, UK: Network Educational Press, 2001), 100.

6. Margaret Cooling, *Creating A Learning Church* (Oxford: BRF, 2005), 80.

7. Eugene H. Peterson, *Christ Plays in Ten Thousand Places*, 30.

8. Gordon Mursell, *The Story of Christian Spirituality* (Oxford: Lion, 2001), 9.

9. Lesslie Newbigin, quoted in Steve Chalke and Simon Johnston, *Faithworks: Intimacy and Involvement* (Eastbourne, UK: Kingsway, 2003), 58.

10. Rowan Williams, quoted in Nick Spencer, *'Doing God': A Future for Faith in the Public Square* (London: Theos, 2006), 32.

11. The origin of the English word *religion* derives from the ancient Latin word *ligare*, which literally meant 'to bind, or connect'. This was prefixed with *re* (again) to form the word *religare* (religion)–'to reconnect'. It refers to 'reconnection' to God, to yourself, to others, to community and to creation. Religion is about a 'calling *to*' something rather than a 'calling *away*' from.

12. Lesslie Newbigin, *The Gospel in a Pluralist Society* (London: SPCK, 1989), 132.

13. Michael Riddell, *The Sacred Journey*: *Reflections on a Life Wholly Lived*, 107.

14. From 'The Second Coming' presented on *Something Understood*, BBC Radio 4, Sunday, 29 June 2008, accessed at *www.bbc.co.uk/radio4/religion/somethingunderstood_20080629.shtml*.

15. John Hayes, cited by Tom Sine, 'The New Conspirators–Modern Monasticism', accessed at *http://msainfo.org/articles/the-new-conspirators-new-monasticism*.

16. Oscar Romero, quoted by Gerard Kelly in *Get a Grip on the Future without Losing Your Hold on the Past* (Oxford: Monarch, 1999), 251. Used with permission.

17. An old Franciscan blessing, quoted in Philip Yancey, *Prayer: Does It Make Any Difference?* (Grand Rapids: Zondervan, 2006).

The Atonement Debate

Papers from the London Symposium on the Theology of Atonement

Derek Tidball and David Hilborn, and Justin Thacker, General Editors

Recent days have seen a debate among evangelicals over how the death of Christ is to be interpreted. When a popular British evangelical leader appeared to denounce the idea that God was punishing Christ in our place on the cross as a 'twisted version of events', 'morally dubious', and a 'huge barrier to faith' that should be rejected in favour of preaching only that God is love, major controversy was stirred.

The public debate which resulted was often heated. In order to act as reconcilers, the Evangelical Alliance and the London School of Theology called for a symposium in which advocates of the different positions could engage with each other. The symposium, which was attended by some 200 participants, was held when the July 7th bombings took place in London and drew together many of Britain's finest evangelical theologians. This book contains the collection of papers given at the symposium, supplemented by a few others for the sake of rounding out the agenda, and grouped in convenient sections.

Softcover: 978-0-310-27339-4

Change Agents

25 Hard-Learned Lessons in the Art of Getting Things Done

Steve Chalke

Change agents are pioneers, entrepreneurs, innovators. They can be difficult, annoying, and demanding. But their calling is demanding too: to take a vision and wrench it into reality.

When Steve Chalke was asked to be the senior minister of a dying inner-city church, he knew what he wanted: to make it into a Christian equivalent of a first-century synagogue. A place where the community gathered, not just to pray and hear sermons, but to be educated, entertained, and to find help.

Making it all happen was the harder part. In *Change Agents*, the author shares twenty-five lessons he learned during this work. He had to teach himself to respond, not react; say no more than yes, give up being everyone's friend, and accept that any success was only a short respite between two crises.

Employing wry humour, personal examples, and a large helping of practical advice, Steve Chalke reminds us our enterprise, not our caution, with the Word of God is what's rewarded. Christ waits and watches for us to take risks and create change in the church, the community and the world at large.

Softcover: 978-0-310-27549-7

Intelligent Church

A Journey Towards Christ-Centred Community

Steve Chalke with Anthony Watkis

> 'Everything that Steve Chalke writes is insightful and cutting-edge. Here he argues in favour of a church that thinks and acts in ways that make the Kingdom of God visible and reasonable in a secular society.'
>
> – Tony Campolo, PhD
> Eastern University, Pennsylvania, USA

The task of the Church is 'to be the irrefutable demonstration and proof of the fact that God is love,' claims Steve Chalke. An intelligent church intentionally connects the Bible and its twenty-first-century culture, is authentic and, most importantly, has thought through its practice. In other words, the way it does church is a reflection of its understanding of who God is.

This foundational issue must be addressed by pastors, church and ministry leaders, small group leaders and others as we continue to grapple with the shape of effective church in the postmodern, post-Christian West.

As Chalke unpacks central theological concepts, such as the incarnation, human sinfulness, and the Trinity, he points us to the corresponding characteristics of an intelligent church, such as inclusiveness, messiness and diversity. Each thought-provoking chapter concludes with a 'Yes but How?' section, which gives practical suggestions for moving your church along this path.

Softcover: 978-0-310-24884-2

Jesus for President

Politics for Ordinary Radicals

Shane Claiborne and Chris Haw

Jesus for President is a radical manifesto to awaken the Christian political imagination, reminding us that our ultimate hope lies not in partisan political options but in Jesus and the incarnation of the peculiar politic of the church as a people 'set apart' from this world.

In what can be termed lyrical theology, *Jesus for President* poetically weaves together words and images to sing (rather than dictate) its message. It is a collaboration of Shane Claiborne's writing and stories, Chris Haw's reflections and research and Chico Fajardo-Heflin's art and design. Drawing upon the work of biblical theologians, the lessons of church history, and the examples of modern-day saints and ordinary radicals, *Jesus for President* stirs the imagination of what the Church could look like if it placed its faith in Jesus instead of Caesar.

A fresh look at Christianity and empire, *Jesus for President* transcends questions of 'Should I vote or not?' and 'Which candidate?' by thinking creatively about the fundamental issues of faith and allegiance. It's written for those who seek to follow Jesus, rediscover the spirit of the early church, and incarnate the kingdom of God.

www.jesusforpresident.org

Softcover: 978-0-310-27842-9
Jesus for President Tour DVD: 978-0-310-32022-7

Jesus Wants to Save Christians

A Manifesto for the Church in Exile

Rob Bell and Don Golden

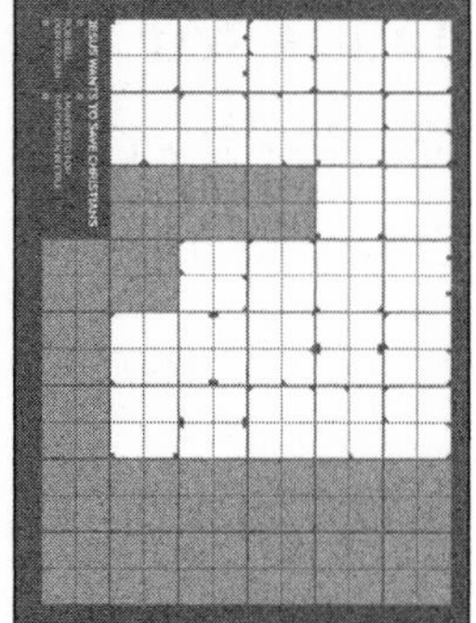

It's a book about faith and fear, wealth and war,poverty, power, safety, terror, Bibles, bombs, and homeland insecurity.

It's about empty empires and the truth that everybody's a priest, it's about oppression, occupation, and what happens when Christians support, animate, and participate in the very things Jesus came to set people free from.

It's about what it means to be a part of the church of Jesus in a world where some people fly planes into buildings while others pick up groceries in Hummers.

www.jesuswantstosavechristians.com

Hardcover, Printed: 978-0-310-27502-2

The Lost Message of Jesus

Steve Chalke and Alan Mann

Who is the real Jesus? Do we remake him in our own image and then wonder why our spirituality is less than life-changing and exciting? Steve Chalke and Alan Mann believe that the real Jesus is deeply challenging. And each new generation must grapple with the question of who he is, because only through a constant study of Jesus are we able to discover God himself.

The Lost Message of Jesus is written to stir thoughtful debate and pose fresh questions that will help create a deeper understanding of Jesus and his message. It is an encounter with the real Jesus of his world—not the Jesus we try to mold to ours. Themes include:

- The Kingdom of God—shalom—is available to everyone now, through Jesus
- The world outside your own church needs to hear of the depth of God's love and suffering
- Jesus was a radical and a revolutionary!
- Jesus offers immediate forgiveness, without cost, to anyone

Focusing on some of the key episodes, events, and issues of Jesus' life, we will see how too often the message we preach today has been influenced more by the culture we live in than the radical, life-changing, world-shaping message Jesus shared two thousand years ago.

Softcover: 978-0-310-24882-8